Vintage Christmas

CRAIG THOMPSON

Vintage Christmas—Christ in the Old Testament

Published by: Ordinary Christian Ministries

Cover Design by: Ginger Chestnut and Courtney Hash

Graphics and designs created in Canva.

ISBN-13:978-1-965968-00-0

Dewey Decimal Classification: 230

Subject Headings: Advent/Devotional Literature/Jesus-Christ-Nativity

Vintage Christmas

CHRIST IN THE OLD TESTAMENT

CRAIG THOMPSON

|ORDINARY|

Contents

Acknowledgments

As always, I am grateful to my Malvern Hill family for the way they support all of my ministry efforts. I am indebted to Ginger Chestnut for her tireless work to make my writing something presentable for the world—her name deserves to be on the cover, but she never puts it there. Luke and Patty Tolbert are two of my favorite people on the planet, and they were willing to read an early copy and give valuable insight—additionally, their years of friendship have fostered many of the seeds that became devotions in this book. Several others were willing to give their time to read all or parts of this book and to help it become what it is today.

This book is the first book published by Ordinary Christian Ministries, which is only possible by the incredible generosity of a donor to whom everyone who reads this book is indebted.

Finally, Angela, Wyatt, Aubrey, Brooklyn, and Sloan always sacrifice when I write. They put up with me listening to Christmas music in the warm spring and summer months as I tried to focus on writing Christmas devotions. They also provide me with love, support, and an endless supply of illustrations. I love them all and am so thankful for the life Angela and I have built together.

Vintage Christmas

CRAIG THOMPSON

Introduction

I hope that your days are merry and bright, and, if I could bring it about, I would ensure that all of your Christmases would be white. I love Christmas, and I love just about everything about it. I love the songs, the food, the lights, the weather, and especially time with family and friends. I love to give and receive gifts, and I eagerly anticipate our family's Christmas Eve candlelight dinner every year.

If you are reading this, there is a good chance that it is nearly Christmas, and you have decided to spend the next few weeks devoting some time and attention to Christ. Most Christmas devotionals are pretty light and fun. In fact, my last Christmas devotion, *Home for the Holidays*, was concise, fun, and focused on getting your household around the table for a brief devotion and time of prayer throughout the Advent season.

In this book, the focus is not so much on family time around the table—though I do hope you will spend time doing devotions with your family this Advent season—but on you growing in your own understanding of this Christ whom we celebrate at Christmas. The birth of Jesus was actually a long-awaited fulfillment of promises that God gave his people hundreds of years before. *Vintage*

Christmas explores Old Testament passages that point to Jesus and will help you to understand the context into which Jesus was born. His birth was prophesied, predicted, foreshadowed, and foretold. Jesus' birth was both necessary and undeserved. The Old Testament points to Jesus, and over the next twenty five days, it is my hope that this book helps you to better see Jesus through the lens of the Old Testament.

Each devotion ends with a question for you to ponder followed by a short prayer. My hope is that, if the goals of this book are met, you will not only celebrate Christmas a little differently this year, but you will also understand your Savior more intimately and learn to love the Bible more fully.

Whether your Christmas is filled with all the trappings of a Christmas song or is celebrated during a bout of unseasonably warm southern weather, I trust that this season will be filled with love and joy as you gather with family and friends to celebrate the birth of our Savior.

God Brings Light

In the beginning, God created the heavens and the earth. The earth was without form and void, and darkness was over the face of the deep. And the Spirit of God was hovering over the face of the waters. And God said, "Let there be light," and there was light. And God saw that the light was good. And God separated the light from the darkness. God called the light Day, and the darkness he called Night. And there was evening and there was morning, the first day.
Genesis 1:1-5

As you begin your Advent journey, you no doubt recognize the need for light. Maybe the darkness of winter reminds you of the need for light, but we also live in a world filled with darkness of many kinds—darkness of depression, doubt, sin, brokenness, and shame. The book of Genesis captures a deeper darkness—darkness without light, an all-encompassing, utter darkness that seems to consume everything. In the beginning there was darkness—until God spoke light into being.

Imagine, a world without light or even the hope or thought of light. For some of you reading this, you have some idea of what that world would be like. Some of you know the power of grief or hurt that pulls you into a dark vortex that seems to give no hope and no light. Some of you have even picked up this book hoping that somehow it could help you to find light in a world that seems incredibly dark in spite of the Christmas lights and decorations around you.

You are not alone. Charles Spurgeon is known as the Prince of Preachers and was the pre-eminent British preacher of the nineteenth century. However, Spurgeon knew well what it was to endure dark nights of the soul. In one sermon he proclaimed,

> *At certain periods clouds and darkness cover the sun, and he beholds no clear shining of the daylight, but walks in darkness and sees no light. Now there are many who have rejoiced in the presence of God for a season; they have basked in the sunshine God has been pleased to give them in the earlier stages of their*

Christian career; they have walked along the "green pastures," by the side of the "still waters," and suddenly—in a month or two—they find that glorious sky is clouded: instead of "green pastures," they have to tread the sandy desert; in the place of "still waters," they find streams brackish to their taste and bitter to their spirits, and they say, "Surely, if I were a child of God this would not happen." Oh! say not so, thou who art walking in darkness. The best of God's saints have their nights; the dearest of his children have to walk through a weary wilderness. There is not a Christian who has enjoyed perpetual happiness, there is no believer who can always sing a song of joy. It is not every lark that can always carol. It is not every star that can always be seen.[1]

The Book of Genesis declares the works of God from the beginning. In the very beginning of all things, God spoke light into the world. Before he even created his people, he illuminated their days. But it was not only in the beginning that God spoke light and offered hope; the very act of creation speaks to the future work of God in Christ. The God who gave light in the darkness of his primitive creation would send the light of the world, Christ, to bring hope into spiritual darkness.

The light of day was good, but the light of Christ is

---

[1] Charles Spurgeon, "The Desire of the Soul in Spiritual Darkness," https:// archive. Spurgeon.org/sermons/0031.php.

better. The light of Christ redeemed creation. As you reflect on Christmas, perhaps you know something of the darkness of sin and shame. Maybe as a follower of Jesus, you even know something of the darkness of the soul that can seem to come from nowhere. In the midst of that darkness, it can be difficult to not be fearful and depressed, but take heart today. The God who brought light in the beginning has sent light again. The light of Christ may seem to be darkened in your life today, but know that the light is there even if you cannot feel its warmth or see its glow. In the deep darkness of winter, you can take heart knowing that the sun has not died, and its light has not gone out. Dark as the nights may seem, morning will come, and eventually spring will return.

In what ways do you struggle to believe the light of Jesus is enough to overcome the darkness in your own life or in the world?

Prayer: God give me eyes to see the darkness around me, and the courage to share the hope of the gospel. Grant me grace to live in your light and to be the light for the world around me.

Water From the Rock

All the congregation of the people of Israel moved on from the wilderness of Sin[1] by stages, according to the commandment of the Lord, and camped at Rephidim, but there was no water for the people to drink. Therefore the people quarreled with Moses and said, "Give us water to drink." And Moses said to them, "Why do you quarrel with me? Why do you test the Lord?" But the people thirsted there for water, and the people grumbled against Moses and said, "Why did you bring us up out of Egypt, to kill us and our children and our livestock with thirst?" So Moses cried to the Lord, "What shall I do with this people? They are almost ready to stone me." And the Lord said

---

[1] The wilderness of Sin is a desert area between Elim and Sinai. See Exodus 16:1.

to Moses, "Pass on before the people, taking with you some of the elders of Israel, and take in your hand the staff with which you struck the Nile, and go. Behold, I will stand before you there on the rock at Horeb, and you shall strike the rock, and water shall come out of it, and the people will drink." And Moses did so, in the sight of the elders of Israel. And he called the name of the place Massah and Meribah, because of the quarreling of the people of Israel, and because they tested the Lord by saying, "Is the Lord among us or not?"
Exodus 17:1-7

The Old Testament is more than rules and expectations; it is also a history of God's people, Israel. God's rescue of his people from slavery in Egypt and his deliverance of them to the Promised Land was the most important event in Israel's history. But the Old Testament is not only history, it is also filled with prophecy and with hints about the future work of God through Jesus Christ. One of the ways God foretells Christ's work is through something called *typology* or *symbolism*. Throughout the Old Testament, God uses many *types* or *symbols* that foretell the future work of Jesus Christ.

The event in Exodus 17 of Moses delivering water from the rock at God's command is not only history, it is typology. In this account, the rock is a type of Christ, which means it foreshadows Jesus. As you meditate on Christ this Christmas season through the Old Testament, take time to appreciate God's wisdom in pointing to Christ in all of Scripture.

As the Hebrew people wandered in the wilderness under Moses's leadership, they struggled to trust in God's provision. When life became difficult, they did not lean into the Lord,[2] they grumbled against God and against God's appointed leader. "But God, being rich in mercy, because of the great love with which he loved us"[3] desired to save his people in spite of their hard-heartedness. When they complained, God did not abandon his people, but instead delivered his people yet again.

God commanded Moses to stand before the people of Israel and to strike a rock with his staff. When the rock was struck, the rock would spew forth water. In a desert land, water is not merely refreshment, water is essential for life. Moses struck the rock and the people were given life. Paul makes it clear in 1 Corinthians 10:4 that the rock represented Christ: "For they drank from the spiritual Rock that followed them, and the Rock was Christ."

The rock yielded life to God's people in the wilderness, and likewise Christ would yield life to God's people who groaned under the darkness of sin and shame. Like the rock, it would be necessary for Christ to be struck so that his people might receive the living water that only he

---

[2] When you read Lord in the Old Testament in upper case, it is a substitute for the proper Hebrew name of God Yahweh, sometimes spelled Jehovah.
[3] Ephesians 2:4

could provide[4]. The Hebrew people in Exodus were on the edge of death and needed water. Jesus came to give life to a people who were already dead in their sins and trespasses, but it was necessary that Christ the Rock suffer and die so that his people could have that life. 1 Peter 2:24 clarifies, "He himself bore our sins in his body on the tree, that we might die to sin and live to righteousness. By his wounds you have been healed."

The life-giving rock in the book of Exodus foreshadows a greater gift to come. Just as it was God's will for the rock to be struck, so, too would it be God's will to "crush him."[5] Jesus was born to die so that all who would call upon him might have life. Just as God desired to deliver the nation of Israel into the promised land in spite of their grumbling, so, too, God desires to deliver his people into their promised rest through Christ in spite of their sin. Jesus came to earth as a human to be crushed for your transgressions so that you might experience the life-giving power of salvation.

This Christmas, celebrate Christ by joyfully receiving the gift he came to bring.

---

[4] John 7:38
[5] Isaiah 53:10

How have you seen God work in spite of your sin?

Prayer: God, thank you for sending Jesus while I was still a sinner. Thank you for giving me living water, even when I did not deserve it.

Passover

These are the appointed feasts of the L<small>ORD</small>, the holy convocations, which you shall proclaim at the time appointed for them. In the first month, on the fourteenth day of the month at twilight, is the L<small>ORD</small>'s Passover. And on the fifteenth day of the same month is the Feast of Unleavened Bread to the L<small>ORD</small>; for seven days you shall eat unleavened bread. On the first day you shall have a holy convocation; you shall not do any ordinary work. But you shall present a food offering to the L<small>ORD</small> for seven days. On the seventh day is a holy convocation; you shall not do any ordinary work.

Leviticus 23:4-8

Moses is the author of the first five books of the Bible: Genesis, Exodus, Leviticus, Numbers, and Deuteronomy. Leviticus, the third of these books, serves to help a redeemed people understand how to live as the holy people of God through obedience and sacrifice. As much as anything, Leviticus shows the people of God that holiness is not an attainable goal outside of God's willingness to forgive through sacrifices and offerings.

Leviticus outlines a system of festivals, sabbaths, and sacrifices the Israelites are expected to cling to as God's people. The sacrificial system of Israel was instituted by God to remind the people of the great cost of their sin and to create a system of atonement whereby the people of Israel might be cleansed. The sabbaths and festivals served as times of solemn rest during which the Israelites were to do no work, but rather worship God, and remember all that he had done on their behalf.

Perhaps no festival or feast in ancient Israel was more important than the Passover (also called the Feast of Unleavened Bread). The Feast of Unleavened Bread was a time to remember and reflect upon God's deliverance of Israel from Egypt's bondage. When Pharaoh refused God's command to let his people go, God acted to force Pharaoh's hand. The tenth plague enacted on the people of Egypt was the plague of the death of the firstborn.[1]

---

[1] Exodus 11-12

Because Pharaoh refused to honor God, God warned that he would kill the firstborn from every household in Egypt. However, he promised to spare the children of Israel. After Pharaoh's final refusal, Moses led Israel to honor God's command. Their instructions on that day were to sacrifice a lamb and eat it together with their household. The blood of the lamb was then to be used to paint the doorposts of houses. When the Angel of the LORD saw the blood on the houses of God's people, he "passed over" those houses, and all individuals inside the home were allowed to live.

The Feast of Unleavened Bread was to serve as a yearly reminder of God's passing over his people. The blood of the lamb also served as a yearly reminder that the death of an innocent lamb was necessary to preserve the lives of all inside a household. When Adam and Eve sinned in the garden and discovered their nakedness, God in his grace sacrificed an animal to make clothes for them to cover their sin.[2] From that time on, death was necessary to atone for (cover) sin. In the case of the Passover, the death of a lamb was even necessary to protect Israel from sins committed against them.

The tenth plague promised in Exodus 11:5 was that, "every firstborn in the land of Egypt shall die." Israel dwelled in the land of Egypt, not by their own desires,

---

[2] Genesis 3:21

but by the sinful decrees of an enemy of God. Israel found itself in a precarious situation, in danger because of the sins of another. God made a way for Israel to be saved—a lamb was slain so that Israel might be saved from the consequences of another's sin.

The imagery is not difficult to connect to Jesus. The book of Revelation often pictures Jesus as a lamb, and in the King James Version, he is even referred to as the "Lamb slain from the foundation of the world" (Revelation 13:8 KJV). The Passover lamb is a symbol pointing forward to Jesus Christ. Jesus died so that punishment could pass over guilty sinners. Jesus also died to deliver his children from the pain and captivity of the sins committed against them.

How has God passed over your sin to bring you to salvation?

Prayer: God, give me grace to be patient with the sins of others as I pray for their salvation.

Cities of Refuge

And the Lord spoke to Moses, saying, "Speak to the people of Israel and say to them, 'When you cross the Jordan into the land of Canaan, then you shall select cities to be cities of refuge for you, that the manslayer who kills any person without intent may flee there. The cities shall be for you a refuge from the avenger, that the manslayer may not die until he stands before the congregation for judgment. And the cities that you give shall be your six cities of refuge. You shall give three cities beyond the Jordan, and three cities in the land of Canaan, to be cities of refuge. These six cities shall be for refuge for the people of Israel, and for the stranger and for

the sojourner among them, that anyone who kills any person
without intent may flee there.'"
Numbers 35:9-15

In 1948, the General Assembly of the United Nations signed the Universal Declaration of Human Rights. Article 11 of that document declares, "Everyone charged with a penal offense has the right to be presumed innocent until proven guilty." Even though the idea of presumed innocence is evident in many places throughout western legal history, the adoption of the Universal Declaration of Human Rights is the first place where "innocent until proven guilty" is clearly spelled out in black and white.

The date above gives a hint as to why it was deemed necessary at that time to spell out human rights in a very clear way. Following World War II, as the atrocities of Nazi Germany became fully apparent, it was essential to clearly identify human rights. Even as Nazi war criminals were tried for their involvement in the holocaust, the responsibility was on the prosecution to prove guilt. Guilt must be proven, not presumed.

The fact that presumed innocence was not enshrined until such a recent date should give you a window into how radical this idea was. In fact, ten members of the United Nations either abstained from voting or neglected to vote at all.

For most of human history, the rule of law did not prevail. As a result, a man (or woman) accused of a crime was often without recourse. Heinous crimes, such as murder, were often adjudicated by family members or mob violence.

The Old Testament, however, provided a recourse for a person who killed another. Murder is, of course, a terrible crime, but not every death is the result of murder. A person could be killed in an accident or even in self-defense. In the case of accidental death or death as a result of self-defense, under Old Testament law, the person responsible for the death of another should not be punished as a murderer. To protect the manslayer, God provided cities of refuge.

These cities were not sanctuary cities to avoid legal judgment; rather, they were places of temporary safety until a manslayer could stand trial. In these cities of refuge, a man could hide from family or friends seeking revenge for the death of their loved ones. Until such time as the death could be investigated, a man's life could be preserved and, if found innocent of murder, even saved.

The cities of refuge in the Old Testament point toward Jesus as our great City of Refuge. Cities of refuge were for those who were innocent, but Ephesians 2 makes it clear that in sin, all people follow after the ruler of the kingdom of this world. In our natural sinful state, all people belong to Satan, but Jesus is the place of refuge where people can flee from their sins. Christ is a refuge even for the guilty. Psalm 46:1 says, "God is our refuge and strength, a very present help in trouble." He is your refuge where you can flee, and the Old Testament cities of refuge are a picture of the greater hope that is found in Jesus Christ.

How have you found Jesus to be a safe place?

Prayer: God, thank you for providing a refuge in Jesus. Help me to trust you to keep me safe amid the struggles and trials of life.

A Chosen People

For you are a people holy to the Lord your God. The Lord your God has chosen you to be a people for his treasured posses- sion, out of all the peoples who are on the face of the earth. It was not because you were more in number than any other people that the Lord set his love on you and chose you, for you were the fewest of all peoples, but it is because the Lord loves you and is keeping the oath that he swore to your fathers, that the Lord has brought you out with a mighty hand and redeemed you from the house of slavery, from the hand of Pharaoh king of Egypt. Know therefore that the Lord your God is God, the faithful God who keeps covenant and steadfast love with those who love him and keep his commandments, to a thousand generations, and repays to their face those

who hate him, by destroying them. He will not be slack with
one who hates him. He will repay him to his face. You shall
therefore be careful to do the commandment and the statutes
and the rules that I command you today.
Deuteronomy 7:6-11

On the night of Jesus' birth, angels appeared in the night sky and announced the good news of great joy to shepherds gathered in a field. The angels promised great joy for all the people, but they went on in Luke 2:14 to exclaim,

> *Glory to God in the highest, and on earth peace among*
> *those with whom he is pleased.*

The Bible is one unified story of God's creation, man's rebellion, and God's redemption. From Genesis to Revelation, God writes the story of his interaction with his creation. The God of Deuteronomy is the God of Luke, which is why we can speak of Christmas from the Old Testament. The book of Deuteronomy is full of laws and rules, but it is wrong to view it narrowly as a rule book. Deuteronomy is a series of sermons preached by Moses to the children of Israel before his death.

Deuteronomy is less of a rule book and more of a code of living for God's people. Some have even spoken of Deuteronomy as a sort of motivational sermon given to Israel to help them understand how to live as God's people. In this context, we discover that Israel is unique as they have been chosen to be God's people on earth—to experience his rule and his blessing and to proclaim his goodness and glory to all the world. God gives them Deuteronomy so they know what he has done for them and what he desires them to do in response.

Jesus, in many ways, is the personification and perfection of the book of Deuteronomy. Moses told the people that they were God's people, and explained how they should live as such. Israel failed in their task, but Jesus lived and died to set up the church as his kingdom on earth. God chose them, but rather than making his glory known, Israel continually worshiped idols and refused to bring others into God's kingdom.

The book of Deuteronomy told God's people how to live, Jesus showed them how to live, and then, when they failed, Jesus chose to die so that they did not have to. Just as God's voice thundered over Mt. Sinai when the written Word was pronounced, God's voice thundered over the river Jordan when the living Word was baptized. God's voice made mountains tremble when the law was instituted, and his voice made hearts shudder when the ministry of Jesus was inaugurated.

But what of those with whom he is "well pleased?" How does Israel relate to those spoken of in Luke 2:14?

Who are God's people today? God's people are Jesus' people. God's chosen people, his treasured possession, are those who are a part of Christ's family—the church. Deuteronomy is a sort of motivational sermon, but one we struggle to obey. Jesus came, not primarily to give a sermon but to be the obedience that God demands. Israel failed repeatedly, but Jesus continues to be victorious. The beloved Son of God is not a motivational sermon. He is life and he is breath. He is salvation to all who call upon his name.

Those with whom God is well-pleased are those for whom Jesus died and who have put their trust in him. Jesus is our perfect peace. He is the fulfillment of all of God's commands. He is your hope!

If you have ever felt left out, the idea of God's exclusivity may feel daunting. You may read the words of Deuteronomy and think, "Well, that's nice, but I wasn't there and no one has chosen me." The great news of the gospel is wrapped up in the promise of Romans 10:13, "Everyone who calls on the name of the LORD will be saved." In *words*, you too can become one of God's chosen people. In *Jesus*, he has chosen all who would call on him for salvation. The moment you give your life to Jesus, you become one of those with whom God is well-pleased. You become a part of God's chosen people, and all of God's promises are true for you!

Does your reading of the Bible cause you to feel left out or included? How does the gospel give you hope to be part of God's family?

Prayer: God, thank you that, in Christ, you have chosen all who will call upon Jesus for salvation. Thank you for my salvation and the hope I can have for others when I share the gospel.

The Scarlet Thread

Then she let them down by a rope through the window, for her house was built into the city wall, so that she lived in the wall. And she said to them, "Go into the hills, or the pursuers will encounter you, and hide there three days until the pursuers have returned. Then afterward you may go your way." The men said to her, "We will be guiltless with respect to this oath of yours that you have made us swear. Behold, when we come into the land, you shall tie this scarlet cord in the window through which you let us down, and you shall gather into your house your father and mother, your brothers, and all your father's household. Then if anyone goes out of the doors of your house into the street, his blood shall be on his own head, and we shall be guiltless. But if a hand is laid on anyone who

is with you in the house, his blood shall be on our head. But if
you tell this business of ours, then we shall be guiltless with
respect to your oath that you have made us swear." And she
said, "According to your words, so be it." Then she sent them
away, and they departed. And she tied the scarlet cord in the
window.
Joshua 2:15-21

The story of Rahab is a story that only God's love could write. Rahab was a prostitute who became a sort of secret agent for the Israelites when they invaded the city of Jericho. The fact that she aided God's people and that He preserved her life would be story enough, but the story does not end there. Rahab is adopted into the nation of Israel as an equal.

Eventually, Rahab marries a man named Salmon and gives birth to a son named Boaz. Boaz will become the father of a man named Obed, and Obed will father Jesse, who is the father of David. David was Israel's greatest king, and Jesus Christ is the fulfillment of God's promises to David. In short, all of that means that a prostitute from Jericho named Rahab is named among the family tree of Jesus Christ in Matthew 1:5.

But why?

The answer is the scarlet thread mentioned in the verses above. The scarlet thread is an allusion to blood.

Just a few days ago, you read that the Israelites smeared blood on the doorposts of their home as a sign for the LORD to pass over their homes when the firstborn children of Egypt were killed. In a similar vein, Rahab was instructed to hang a scarlet cord from her window so that the armies of Israel would pass over her home.

As New Testament Christians, we know that the cord was more than an allusion to the Passover. The cord of Rahab represented the blood of Jesus Christ and pointed forward toward a greater sacrifice that was to come.

Adrian Rogers speaks of the scarlet thread through Scripture this way,

> *From the very beginning of human history, it is revealed. When Adam and Eve sinned, God shed innocent blood in order to make them clothes from animal skins (Genesis 3:21). This is a picture of the covering of righteousness that we receive when the LORD Jesus Christ died for us.*
>
> *In Genesis four we read that Adam and Eve had two sons, Cain and Abel. They instinctively wanted to worship God. Cain sacrificed the fruit of the ground. Abel had already learned that God demanded blood, so he brought a lamb. God accepted the blood of Abel's lamb, but He did not accept Cain's offering. Why? Because "without the shedding of blood, there is no remission of sin" (Hebrews 9:22).*

And God told Abraham to sacrifice his long-awaited son Isaac (Genesis 22). Just before Abraham plunged the dagger into the quivering heart of his son, an angel stopped him. Abraham saw a ram caught in a thicket. Isaac was set free, but an innocent animal's blood was shed instead.

Then, God wanted to deliver His people from bondage in the land of Egypt. On the night of the Passover, God instructed each house to slay a lamb and put the blood on their door. God said in Exodus 12:13, "When I see the blood, I will pass over you."

And in the tabernacle and later in the temple, thousands upon thousands of sheep, oxen, and turtle doves were killed and their blood spilt as sacrifices for sin.

And finally, the Lord Jesus Christ died upon the cross. His death was the fulfillment of all the prophecy and promises. Revelation 13:8 proclaims that He was slain before the foundation of the world. He came to die; He planned to die; He lived to die; and He was born to die.

Blood is throughout Scripture, but what does Christ's blood mean to us?

Before this planet was ever swung into space, God had determined in His heart that He would send His Son to die upon the cross. How wonderful it is to trace the scarlet thread of the blood of Christ woven throughout the Bible! How much more wonderful to experience its *redemption personally. Praise God for the blood of His Lamb![1]*

Rahab was saved from death because she was covered by the scarlet cord that hung from her window. Christians are saved from eternal death because they have been saved by the scarlet thread of Christ's blood that flowed down the cross of Calvary.

In what ways does the New Testament help you to better understand the Old Testament?

Prayer: Thank you, God, for having a plan for me, and for the whole of humanity, before the world was ever created.

[1] Rogers, Adrian. "The Scarlet Thread Through the Bible." The Scarlet Thread through the Bible - Love Worth Finding with Adrian Rogers, 2021, www.oneplace.com/ministries/love-worth-finding/read/articles/scarlet-thread-through-the-bible-10591.html.

There Was No King

In those days there was no king in Israel. Everyone did what was right in his own eyes.
Judges 21:25

The book of Judges ends with a judgment against God's people. Everyone did what was right in his own eyes. Notice, the Bible does not say that everyone did what was right in his own eyes because there was no king. It could be easy to misread the text this way, but the fact that there was no king in Israel is not given as an excuse for why the Israelites did whatever they wanted to do.

There was no king in Israel because God set himself

up as the king over Israel. There was no king, but there was law and there was instruction. There was no king, but God had spoken. Most famously, God spoke from Mt. Sinai with the Ten Commandments. Just consider God's Words from Exodus 20:1-17:

> And God spoke all these words, saying, "I am the Lord your God, who brought you out of the land of Egypt, out of the house of slavery. You shall have no other gods before me. You shall not make for yourself a carved image, or any likeness of anything that is in heaven above, or that is in the earth beneath, or that is in the water under the earth. You shall not bow down to them or serve them, for I the Lord your God am a jealous God, visiting the iniquity of the fathers on the children to the third and the fourth generation of those who hate me, but showing steadfast love to thousands of those who love me and keep my commandments. You shall not take the name of the Lord your God in vain, for the Lord will not hold him guiltless who takes his name in vain. Remember the Sabbath day, to keep it holy. Six days you shall labor, and do all your work, but the seventh day is a Sabbath to the Lord your God. On it you shall not do any work, you, or your son, or your daughter, your male servant, or your female servant, or your livestock, or the sojourner who is within your gates. For in six days the Lord made heaven and earth, the sea, and all that is in them, and rested on the seventh day. Therefore the Lord

blessed the Sabbath day and made it holy. Honor your
father and your mother, that your days may be long in
the land that the Lord your God is giving you. You shall
not murder. You shall not commit adultery. You shall
not steal. You shall not bear false witness against your
neighbor. You shall not covet your neighbor's house; you
shall not covet your neighbor's wife, or his male servant,
or his female servant, or his ox, or his donkey, or any-
thing that is your neighbor's.

There was no king in Israel, but there was a God who
had spoken to his people. And yet, his people ignored his
commands. The children of Israel had been rescued from
Egypt with God's mighty hand and had been delivered
into the land of promise. Once they began to settle in the
promised land, they promptly forgot their God and his
expectations for them.

But God did not forget them. The book of Judges
paints a picture of a lawless people, but a gracious
God who continues to deliver them in spite of their
hard-heartedness. The people do what they want, and
though God would be justified in leaving them to their
own sinful devices, God continues to send judges (military
leaders), provided by God's grace, to protect and deliver
the people from foreign oppressors. God's people were
disobedient and faithless, but God was faithful to send

redeemers (a person responsible to restore the rights of another) over and over again.

The book of Judges points toward God's great mercy in Jesus. Romans 5:8 says, "God shows his love for us in that while we were still sinners, Christ died for us." Just as God showed his love to a rebellious people over and over again in the book of Judges, God has shown his love toward sinners by sending Jesus to die. Redeemer judges like Samson, Deborah, and Gideon were flawed people who led God's people for a particular time and purpose. Jesus is the greater and perfect judge who never fails. Jesus offers eternal redemption.

Jesus is the king the people of Judges did not know they needed, and he is the perfect redemption we could have only hoped for.

Obedience can come across to some as a bad word. How does obedience become easier knowing that Jesus is the king to whom you owe respect?

Prayer: Father, help me to have an obedient heart to your rule and reign. Help me to see your kingship as a comfort rather than a burden.

Flight From God's Blessing

So the two of them went on until they came to Bethlehem. And
when they came to Bethlehem, the whole town was stirred
because of them. And the women said, "Is this Naomi?" She
said to them, "Do not call me Naomi; call me Mara, for the
Almighty has dealt very bitterly with me. I went away full, and
the Lord has brought me back empty. Why call me Naomi,
when the Lord has testified against me and the Almighty has
brought calamity upon me?" So Naomi returned, and Ruth
the Moabite her daughter-in-law with her, who returned from

the country of Moab. And they came to Bethlehem at the
beginning of barley harvest.
Ruth 1:19-22

The story of Naomi's return to Bethlehem with her daughter-in-law Ruth is well known. What often gets lost in the Ruth story is the beginning of the book. The book of Ruth does not begin with Ruth. The book of Ruth begins in the time of the Judges with a man named Elimelech, his wife, Naomi, and their two sons, Mahlon and Chilion. Elimelech was from Bethlehem—the same Bethlehem that would be the birthplace of Jesus. A famine occurred in the land, during which Elimelech and his family left Bethlehem and journeyed into the country of Moab.

A little background is beneficial here. First, you need to know that the word Bethlehem is a compound Hebrew word that literally means *house of bread*. Bethlehem was a city located in the land God had promised to his followers. Elimelech lived in the breadbasket of God's Promised Land. When the famine came to the land, Elimelech left the Promised Land and journeyed to Moab.

> *In the days when the judges ruled there was a famine*
> *in the land, and a man of Bethlehem in Judah went*
> *to sojourn in the country of Moab, he and his wife and*
> *his two sons. The name of the man was Elimelech and*
> *the name of his wife Naomi, and the names of his two*
> *sons were Mahlon and Chilion. They were Ephrathites*

from Bethlehem in Judah. They went into the country of Moab and remained there. But Elimelech, the husband of Naomi, died, and she was left with her two sons.
Ruth 1:1-3

Moab was not a part of God's Promised Land. Actually, the Moabites were more like the antithesis of God's plan for his people. While God's people wandered in the wilderness, the book of Numbers recounts that the people of Moab enticed Israel to worship false gods.

While Israel lived in Shittim, the people began to whore with the daughters of Moab. These invited the people to the sacrifices of their gods, and the people ate and bowed down to their gods. So Israel yoked himself to Baal of Peor. And the anger of the Lord was kindled against Israel.
Numbers 25:1-3

Elimelech lived in the middle of God's promise, but when life became difficult, Elimelech, Naomi, and their two sons fled from God's promise in order to seek out blessing in the land of Moab. A land dominated by idolatry.

Elimelech's story is reminiscent of the Prodigal Son whom Jesus will teach about in the New Testament in Luke 15. Elimelech's story is surely familiar to many who will read these pages. When the storms of life hit, Elimelech and Naomi did not draw near to the LORD, instead they ran from the LORD.

Of course, this is not where the book of Ruth ends. In fact, that is just the first three verses of the book. The book of Ruth goes on to recount how Naomi's sons married foreign women, and then Naomi's husband and two sons died leaving three widows to fend for themselves. Recognizing her desperate situation, Naomi resolves to go home to Bethlehem, and Ruth commits to stay with her mother-in-law.

Where do we see allusions to Christ in all of this mess? If you continue to read the book of Ruth, you will see that there are strong allusions to Christ in the story of Ruth's redeemer, Boaz. Just as Boaz redeemed Ruth, Christ came to redeem his people.

As you consider Christmas this year, perhaps you have spent some time wandering far from God's blessings. Maybe you have journeyed to a far land, fleeing from God's promises and blessings. The book of Ruth shows a beautiful picture of God's grace and kindness.

Naomi had fled from God's promise and sought out blessing in an idolatrous land, but God did not move away from Naomi. Naomi left Bethlehem, but Bethlehem did not move. When Naomi was ready to turn her eyes back to the land of God's blessing, God was willing to welcome her back in. After turning her back on God and his people, there was still a place for Naomi.

There is still room for you. No matter how far you have fled, no matter what country or false hope you have journeyed into, Bethlehem is still waiting for you to come home. The God who welcomed back Naomi and created a way for Ruth, the woman of Moab, to be welcomed into God's people is the same God who will welcome you. Like the Father in Jesus' parable of the Prodigal Son, God is ready to bless you and take you into his home.

When has Jesus been a safe place for you to run after wandering away from his blessings?

Prayer: Dear Lord, keep me near to your place of promise and blessing and protect me from my sinful wanderings. Thank you for your grace in welcoming me back when I have sought security in people and things other than you.

A Forever Kingdom

"When your days are fulfilled and you lie down with your fathers, I will raise up your offspring after you, who shall come from your body, and I will establish his kingdom. He shall build a house for my name, and I will establish the throne of his kingdom forever. I will be to him a father, and he shall be to me a son. When he commits iniquity, I will discipline him with the rod of men, with the stripes of the sons of men, but my steadfast love will not depart from him, as I took it from Saul, whom I put away from before you. And your house and your kingdom shall be made sure forever before me. Your throne shall be established forever." In accordance with all

these words, and in accordance with all this vision, Nathan
spoke to David.
2 Samuel 7:12-17

The books of Judges and Ruth do more than tell us about God's deliverance and redemption. They also provide a background for the lack of leadership in Israel, a genealogy of King David, and ultimately the genealogy of Jesus.

In Judges and Ruth, there was no king in Israel and the people longed for a king like the other nations around them.[1] At this point in Israel's history, they were being governed and led by priests and judges, but Israel wanted more. They were not interested in God's rule or even in God's chosen ruler. Israel wanted to be respected among their peers—they wanted a king like the kings of other nations.

God gave Israel exactly what they wanted. 1 Samuel records the beginning of Israel's monarchy. They wanted a king, so God provided Saul, a man who looked like a king. He was an outspoken leader, he was handsome, he was tall, and he was a capable warrior.[2] They believed that Saul was the man who would make Israel a respectable kingdom and would give them peace from their adversaries, but the reign of Saul did not turn out so well. In fact, it did

---

[1] 1 Samuel 8:5
[2] 1 Samuel 9:2

not even begin well. In 1 Samuel 10:20-24, as Samuel was proclaiming Saul the king of Israel, Saul was hiding among the baggage.

Saul began his reign as king by hiding from leadership and ended his reign by refusing to honor God and falling on his own sword.[3] Saul did not respect his people, and Saul was a suspicious and paranoid leader. When confronted by the giant Goliath, Saul saw the enemy of God's people, but he did not trust in the power of God to deliver his people.[4] When blessed with a soldier named David, Saul saw only competition, not camaraderie.[5]

The people should not have been surprised. God warned them in 1 Samuel 8 that their king would not satisfy them. He would lay heavy burdens on them and they would grow to loathe their decision. But, like so many others before and after them, the Israelites were hard-headed and hard-hearted. The Israelites trusted their own desires and their own wisdom more than the Word of God.

In spite of their disregard for God and his Word, God was merciful and gracious to his people. Israel chose to follow after the nations around them, but God had chosen Israel. God's people rejected his guidance, but God did not reject his people—neither did he abandon them. In

---

[3] 1 Samuel 31:5
[4] 1 Samuel 17:8-1
[5] 1 Samuel 18:6-11

the middle of their rebellion, God sent an answer and a promise.

The answer God gave to his people was his king. He sent them David, a man after his own heart, who would lead God's people as God would have them be led. He would send them a king who would love them as a shepherd loves his sheep. However, even this great king would fail. David sinned greatly, but God's goodness toward Israel was greater than David's failure.

David was the king Gods' people needed at that time, but God would do even more than meet Israel's immediate need. God used David to establish a kingly line that ultimately produced a king unlike any other—King Jesus.

God's people chose Saul, a king in their image who would help them to be like the nations around them. But God promised a king to come—a Messiah who would make Israel different from the nations around them. Israel would become a nation of priests offering salvation to all.

The line of David culminates in Jesus, the great King in God's image who would provide for his people and lead them out of their sin and shame. Just as God sent David to a people who did not ask for him or deserve him, God has sent Jesus to a people who were lost in their sin and rebellion.

How has God shown grace or mercy in your life when you least deserved it or expected it?

Prayer: God, thank you for sending the Savior we needed, even when we did not know how to want him. Thank you for loving me while I was still a sinner.

God Takes Our Sin

Then Elijah said to all the people, "Come near to me." And all the people came near to him. And he repaired the altar of the LORD that had been thrown down. Elijah took twelve stones, according to the number of the tribes of the sons of Jacob, to whom the word of the LORD came, saying, "Israel shall be your name," and with the stones he built an altar in the name of the LORD. And he made a trench about the altar, as great as would contain two seahs of seed. And he put the wood in order and cut the bull in pieces and laid it on the wood. And he said, "Fill four jars with water and pour it on the burnt offering and on the wood." And he said, "Do it a second time." And they did it a second time. And he said, "Do it a third time." And they did it a third time. And the water ran around the

altar and filled the trench also with water. And at the time
of the offering of the oblation, Elijah the prophet came near
and said, "O Lord, God of Abraham, Isaac, and Israel, let it be
known this day that you are God in Israel, and that I am your
servant, and that I have done all these things at your word.
Answer me, O Lord, answer me, that this people may know
that you, O Lord, are God, and that you have turned their
hearts back." Then the fire of the Lord fell and consumed the
burnt offering and the wood and the stones and the dust, and
licked up the water that was in the trench. And when all the
people saw it, they fell on their faces and said, "The Lord, he is
God; the Lord, he is God."
1 Kings 18:30-39d

When John the Baptist saw Jesus approaching him, he announced, "Behold, the Lamb of God, who takes away the sin of the world!"[1] Imagine hearing for the very first time that there was someone who could take away sin. If you have been a Christian for a long time, it is possible that you have begun to take that idea for granted. You know what Jesus did and it can cease to amaze you. Like many other things, it can even begin to seem ordinary.

John Bunyan once wrote, "The man who does not know the nature of the law cannot know the nature of sin. And he who does not know the nature of sin cannot

---

[1] John 1:29

53

know the nature of the Savior."[2] Imagine knowing you are a sinner and that your sin has created separation from God without the hope of a Savior. Imagine knowing you are drowning in your sin and shame and living with constant fear of eternal damnation. How would you respond to learning of a Lamb who could wipe away sin?

In the story of Elijah, the people of Israel knew that they were living under God's judgment. They languished under a drought that had lingered for three years. They depended on water for everything. Water was life, and they had none. They were under judgment because of their sin and the sins of their leaders.

In this place of desperation, they sought hope and help from Baal, the pagan god of rain and fertility. Of course, their desperate attempt to find rain from Baal only further alienated them from Yahweh, the one true and living God. In this situation, one could hardly blame the LORD if he were to turn his back on Israel and leave them to perish under the worship of a false god.

As you have already seen repeatedly in this study of the Old Testament, God is merciful. The story of Elijah shows how willing God is to take away the sin of his people. When Elijah confronts the prophets of Baal on Mt. Carmel, he

---

[2] Bunyan, John. "The Doctrine of the Law and Grace Unfolded." Acacia John Bunyan - Online Library - Sermons & Allegories - the Doctrine of the Law and Grace Unfolded: Epistle, acacia.pair.com/Acacia.John.Bunyan/Sermons. Allegories/Doctrine.Law.Grace/Epistle.to.the.Reader.html.

does not come by invitation. Elijah shows up uninvited and challenges the prophets of Baal to a contest to see who will answer by fire, Baal or Yahweh.

The situation is dire for God's people. The altar to Yahweh has been torn down, and, before Elijah can even offer a sacrifice, it is necessary that the altar be repaired. Twelve stones are used to represent the original twelve tribes of Israel. Then the meat for the sacrifice is laid carefully on the altar, and, finally, Elijah commands that twelve jars of water be poured onto the sacrifice before he even begins to pray.

What is the purpose of the water? Surely, one reason for the water is to remove any doubt about the supernatural nature of God answering by fire, but that is not the only purpose. The water poured out also represents the accumulated sin of the nation of Israel. The people prayed to Baal, the Canaanite god of agriculture and fertility, for water. For months, God's people had prayed to an idol for water. For months, God's people had offered false worship to a false god.

When Elijah poured out the water, he was symbolically pouring out the accumulated false prayers of the people on the altar. Elijah was pouring out the sins of God's people on God's altar. And then, the seemingly impossible happened. Not only did water burn, but the sins of God's people were consumed.

They had prayed for Baal to send water. God responded by showing his power over the water they craved. Baal could not send water, but even if he could, the water for which the people prayed could not stop the one true God. The people prayed to Baal for water. Elijah poured out water, and then prayed to Yahweh, the God of Israel to answer by fire. And he did.

God responds to Elijah's prayer by consuming the offering. The fire of God falls and consumes the sacrificed bull, all of the wood, and the water that had flowed off of the sacrifice. The sacrifice was polluted by the sin of God's people, but God accepted their sinful sacrifice and God's fire consumed all of the water as well.

When Jesus died on the cross, he died to atone for the sins of the world. He died to deliver you from the punishment for your sin, but he also died to take away your sin. Just as the fire of God fell and consumed all of the water that ran off Elijah's sacrifice and filled the trench, the death of Jesus results in the complete removal of sin from his children.

What are some ways you can praise the Lord and show gratitude to him for the removal of your sin. How does forgiveness drive you to an attitude of gratitude?

Prayer: Dear God, thank you for loving me more than I could ever deserve and for forgiving me for all of my sin.

A Better Covenant

*And they brought in the ark of God and set it inside the tent
that David had pitched for it, and they offered burnt offerings
and peace offerings before God. And when David had finished
offering the burnt offerings and the peace offerings, he
blessed the people in the name of the LORD and distributed
to all Israel, both men and women, to each a loaf of bread, a
portion of meat, and a cake of raisins.*
1 Chronicles 16:1-3

Every year at Christmas I roll my eyes at the new car
commercials. There is always a tree, some snow, and a
small box. Inside the box is a key. And then, you guessed
it, the husband or wife is escorted outside with the key

to see their new car. The anticipation in the commercial comes from the key inside the little box.

When someone opens a box and discovers a key, they know that the key itself isn't the gift. The real gift is found using the key. The key points to something greater. In the passage above, you read of the ark of God being brought into Jerusalem by David and placed in a special tent that David had pitched to house the ark.

The ark of God is also known as the ark of the covenant or the ark of the testimony. It was a box overlaid in gold with two cherubim on the lid. The ark was about four and a half feet long and about two and a half feet wide. God instructed Moses to have the ark built, and it contained several artifacts from the Israelites' time in the wilderness. Its primary contents were the two stone tablets upon which God had written the Ten Commandments—the covenant of God with Israel; thus it was literally an ark with the covenant inside.

The ark of the covenant represented the presence of God as something like a throne or a footstool. The ark was important for Israel as a constant reminder of God's goodness to them, but in many ways, it was a little like the car key in the Christmas commercials.

The ark was not God, but it pointed to him. The ark was not the heart of God, but it pointed to his love, his faithfulness, and his commitment to Israel. The ark represented God's covenant with Israel, but it also pointed to a greater covenant.

The ark contained a covenant written on tablets of stone, but it pointed to a covenant that would be written on human hearts. Jeremiah promised this very thing in Jeremiah 31:31-33:

> Behold, the days are coming, declares the Lord, when I will make a new covenant with the house of Israel and the house of Judah, not like the covenant that I made with their fathers on the day when I took them by the hand to bring them out of the land of Egypt, my covenant that they broke, though I was their husband, declares the Lord. For this is the covenant that I will make with the house of Israel after those days, declares the Lord: I will put my law within them, and I will write it on their hearts. And I will be their God, and they shall be my people.

The old covenant is important and it matters. It was God's covenant with Israel to care for them—his commitment to be their God and for them to be his people. The old covenant also points to a better covenant—one written on the heart and sealed with the Holy Spirit. The old covenant points toward—and gives way to—a new covenant that cannot be undone.

This Christmas, search your heart, know the love that

God has written there, and rest secure knowing that he has sealed that covenant with the presence of his Holy Spirit in your heart.

How much more difficult would it have been to live a life dedicated to the Lord in Old Testament times without the indwelling of the Holy Spirit and the Holy Spirit's conviction of sin?

Prayer: Lord, thank you for the Holy Spirit who gives me assurance of my salvation and even intercedes in my prayers to you when I do not know what or how to pray.

Though You Were Dead

*In the first year of Cyrus king of Persia, that the word of the
Lord by the mouth of Jeremiah might be fulfilled, the Lord
stirred up the spirit of Cyrus king of Persia, so that he made
a proclamation throughout all his kingdom and also put it
in writing: "Thus says Cyrus king of Persia: The Lord, the God
of heaven, has given me all the kingdoms of the earth, and
he has charged me to build him a house at Jerusalem, which
is in Judah. Whoever is among you of all his people, may his
God be with him, and let him go up to Jerusalem, which is in
Judah, and rebuild the house of the Lord, the God of Israel—
he is the God who is in Jerusalem. And let each survivor, in*

whatever place he sojourns, be assisted by the men of his
place with silver and gold, with goods and with beasts,
besides freewill offerings for the house of God that is in
Jerusalem."
Ezra 1:1-4

What is your favorite part of the Christmas season? Is it the lights or the food? Maybe you love shopping or cookies or candy? For many people, the music of Christmas is one of the highlights. Which is your favorite type of Christmas music—Christmas carols, classic Christmas hits, classical Christmas music, or perhaps newer Christmas music?

Personally, I love it all. I love Christmas carols by candlelight. I listen to Vince Guaraldi's music from *A Charlie Brown Christmas*. My Christmas play list is full of classics like I'm *Dreaming of A White Christmas* and *The Christmas Song*—though I acknowledge hating *I Want A Hippopotamus for Christmas*. As much as I love the nostalgia of old music, I really enjoy seeing new Christmas songs make an impact.

One of my favorite December songs actually has nothing to do with Christmas. In *A Long December*, 90s grunge band, Counting Crows sings,

> *And it's been a long December and there's reason to*
> *believe*
> *Maybe this year will be better than the last*

I can't remember all the times I tried to tell myself
To hold on to these moments as they pass[1]

Some of you know that feeling as Christmas approaches. The dark days are cold and lonely. Perhaps, just a few days into the month, December already feels too long and you are hopeful that next year could bring something better. In the story of Ezra above, the people would have had no reason to hope for something better.

The people of Israel were captives in a foreign land. They had been in captivity for 70 years, and, for many—maybe most—Israelites, the thought that the darkness of their captivity could end was not something they dared to dream. For those who had been born into captivity, they might have even forgotten to hope for freedom or the opportunity to return to their homeland.

But God had not forgotten his people.

In the first year of Cyrus, king of Persia, God moved in the heart of a pagan king to arrange for the return of his people and the rebuilding of his temple in Jerusalem, the capital city of Israel. That dream for which God's people did not even dare hope was realized, but not because of their abilities or their power. God remembered his people in captivity and created a way to bring them home. God

---

[1] Counting Crows. "A Long December." Recovering the Satellites, UMG Recordings, Inc, 1996.

remembered his people who were separated from him because of their sin, and he created a way they could reunite with him in worship, in a house built for God in Jerusalem, by a pagan king.

The first chapter of John teaches that in the person of Jesus Christ, God came down and made his dwelling among his people. Jesus, the living temple of God, came down and lived among his people. God made a way for his people who were living far from him to be rejoined to him in worship and praise.

In the first year of Cyrus's rule, God moved in King Cyrus to bring about the rebuilding of the temple so that the people of God could return to the place of God and experience the presence and rule of God. When it seemed as though hope was lost and could not even be dreamed of, God rebuilt his temple and drew his people toward himself.

In the midst of a dark night God sent his angels to announce the coming of his Christ.[2] In the middle of your long December, there is hope. Hope is found in the Christ who came as the living temple of God to bring salvation and healing to people living far from God in their captivity to sin.

---

[2] Luke 2:8-20

For what are you hoping this December?

Prayer: God, hear my heart and meet me at the point of my need. You know my hopes and dreams. You know my hurts and pains. God, as you have met your people in the past, I trust you to meet me here.

The God Who Hears

As soon as I heard these words I sat down and wept and mourned for days, and I continued fasting and praying before the God of heaven. And I said, "O LORD God of heaven, the great and awesome God who keeps covenant and steadfast love with those who love him and keep his commandments, let your ear be attentive and your eyes open, to hear the prayer of your servant that I now pray before you day and night for the people of Israel your servants, confessing the sins of the people of Israel, which we have sinned against you. Even I and my father's house have sinned. We have acted very corruptly against you and have not kept the commandments, the statutes, and the rules that you commanded your servant Moses. Remember the word that you commanded

your servant Moses, saying, 'If you are unfaithful, I will scatter
you among the peoples, but if you return to me and keep my
commandments and do them, though your outcasts are in the
uttermost parts of heaven, from there I will gather them and
bring them to the place that I have chosen, to make my name
dwell there.' They are your servants and your people, whom
you have redeemed by your great power and by your strong
hand. O Lord, let your ear be attentive to the prayer of your
servant, and to the prayer of your servants who delight to fear
your name, and give success to your servant today,
and grant him mercy in the sight of this man."
Now I was cupbearer to the king.
Nehemiah 1:4-11

There is a story in my wife's family about a family member who struggled with hearing loss but refused to acknowledge it. One evening, a phone call came, and this man called his wife into the room to handle it, saying, "I'm having a hard time hearing. It is Miracle Hill, and I guess they want a donation." Miracle Hill is a local ministry in their town; however, it turns out that the call was from *Miracle Ear*, not Miracle Hill. Miracle Ear was calling to offer their services to anyone with hearing problems. The sweet wife who took the phone promptly informed the caller that they had no need of hearing aids, because everyone in their house could hear just fine.

We laugh about that story, but you may sometimes

feel like your prayers are similar to that phone call. You pray, but it seems that the LORD is like that family member, and he does not hear what you are saying. Or maybe you feel like he just isn't listening.

What kind of prayer does God hear? The story of Nehemiah teaches many things about leadership and God's provision, but it begins with a lesson on prayer. The verses above begin with Nehemiah fasting and praying to the LORD, but what brought about this time of intense prayer? The first three verses of Nehemiah tell about the broken-down state of Jerusalem and the dire position of God's people in Jerusalem:

> *The remnant there in the province who had survived the exile is in great trouble and shame. The wall of Jerusalem is broken down, and its gates are destroyed by fire. Nehemiah 1:3*

When Nehemiah heard these words, his spirit was broken, and he sat down and wept and mourned for days, continuing to fast and pray before the God of heaven.[1] God heard Nehemiah's prayer when Nehemiah realized that God was his only hope. God heard Nehemiah's prayer when Nehemiah prayed in faith and repentance.

Nehemiah prayed for God to keep his covenant and

---

[1] Nehemiah 1:4

restore his people, and God did. But Nehemiah's prayer and God's answer point to a greater answer to come. The same God who kept covenant with his people in the days of Nehemiah was willing to keep his covenant into the New Testament as well. In fact, the God of the Old Testament covenant made a new and better covenant with his own blood. On the night he would die, Jesus told his disciples as they observed the last supper, "This cup that is poured out for you is the new covenant in my blood."[2]

Nehemiah was cupbearer to a king, and he prayed to the God of Old Testament covenant. In Christ, a new cup was to be established and carried, not by a king's servant, but by the King himself.

Nehemiah could have confidence in his prayers because he was praying to the God of covenant. You can have confidence in your prayers because you also pray to the God of covenant, the one who has made his new covenant with his own blood.

[2] Luke 22:20

How do God's actions in the past give you confidence in your prayers today?

Prayer: Lord, sustain me when I feel like my prayers do not make it to you. Help me to trust you in the present because of who you are, and in the future because what you have done.

DAY FOURTEEN

An Arbiter

For he is not a man, as I am, that I might answer him, that we should come to trial together. There is no arbiter between us, who might lay his hand on us both.

Job 9:32-33

Job is one of the oldest books in the Bible. Most scholars believe Job lived during the time of the Patriarchs[1] in the Old Testament. Job was an exceptionally wealthy man with a large family and a seemingly unwavering commitment to the Lord.

---

[1] Patriarchs: especially, Abraham, Isaac, and Jacob

The book of Job begins with Satan opposing the Lord and with Job himself losing nearly everything. Satan attacked Job and took his wealth and his children away from him in one day. Eventually, even Job's health was impacted, yet Job refused to curse the Lord.

Job's friends accused him of heinous sin, and Job's wife encouraged him to turn his back on the Lord, but Job was steadfast, telling his wife, "Shall we receive good from God, and shall we not receive evil?"[2]

Job did not curse the LORD, but Job was honest with him, crying out to God in anger and anguish, often in ways reminiscent of the Psalms. One of Job's most transparent prayers is recorded in Job 9 where Job nearly accuses the LORD of bullying him. He acknowledges God's greatness and his own limited existence. Job confesses that God is holy and great, and that he himself is weak and small.

As Job pours out his complaint, he goes on to admit that even if he stood before the LORD, it would do him no good. What Job needs is an arbiter—someone who could stand between him and the LORD and argue his case on his behalf. In Job 9:33 listed above, you read, "There is no arbiter," but some translators believe it should say, "Would that there were an arbiter."

Job knew what he needed. He knew that he could not

---

[2] Job 2:10

stand up to the Lord. He knew that he needed someone to argue his case on his behalf.

Job needed Jesus.

In his first letter to his young protégé, Timothy, the apostle Paul writes, "For there is one God, and there is one mediator between God and men, the man Christ Jesus, who gave himself as a ransom for all, which is the testimony given at the proper time."[3] Jesus is the mediator that Job longed for.

Job knew he could not stand before the Lord to argue his case. Job acknowledges his weakness and his sin. In Job 9:20 he says, "Though I am in the right, my own mouth would condemn me; though I am blameless, he would prove me perverse." Job recognized that even though he was "blameless" from a human perspective, in the presence of God his sin would be found out.

Job prays for God to hear him and to help him. He knows he needs God to not only hear his prayers, but to make a way for his prayers to be heard. Because Job knows he is helpless, he throws himself on the mercy of God.

Job knew he needed a mediator. God also knew Job needed a mediator, and God knew that only his son would be sufficient. Job did not just need someone to speak on his behalf. Job needed a Savior.

---

[3] 1 Timothy 2:5-6

The need for Christ did not begin when Mary gave birth to Jesus. The need for a Savior has existed since the very beginning of time. Job realized his need, and he cried out for help. From the beginning of the Old Testament to the end, the long shadow of Christ points to the hope that was to be born in a stable in Bethlehem.

What is a mediator, and why is it important that Christ is the mediator between you and the Father?

Prayer: Father, thank you for sending Jesus to bridge the gap between me and you. Thank you that the cross made a way for me to be brought into a right relationship with you.

Forsaken for You

My God, my God, why have you forsaken me? Why are you so
far from saving me, from the words of my groaning?
Psalm 22:1

In the history of all spoken language, perhaps no sentence is as heart-wrenching as Psalm 22:1. Spoken first by the psalmist, David, it was a desperate cry from his heart. David felt abandoned by the LORD. He could not see a way of hope or escape in his situation. The Psalms are filled with gut-level honesty prayed to the LORD, just like this verse.

David was scared and alone and felt utterly forsaken

by the LORD, but as the Psalm continues, David shows that he knows God hears him. He felt forsaken, but he was not.

The prayer of Psalm 22:1 finds its ultimate and most heart-wrenching fulfillment not with David, but with Christ upon the cross.[1] As the weight of the world's sin bears down on Jesus and as the nails of the cross rip at his hands, Jesus faces the greatest punishment of the cross. There, as he hangs in the balance between God and man, Jesus finds himself utterly forsaken by the Father, and he cries out the very words of this Psalm.

Stuart Townsend captures this scene well in the hymn, *How Deep the Father's Love for Us*.[2]

> *How deep the Father's love for us,*
> *How vast beyond all measure,*
> *That He should give His only Son*
> *To make a wretch His treasure.*

> **How great the pain of searing loss –**
> **The Father turns His face away,**
> *As wounds which mar the Chosen One*
> *Bring many sons to glory.*

> *It was my sin that held Him there*
> *Until it was accomplished;*

---

[1] Matthew 27:46
[2] Stuart Townsend, "How Deep the Father's Love," 2006, Integrity Music.

His dying breath has brought me life –
I know that it is finished.

I will not boast in anything,
No gifts, no power, no wisdom;
But I will boast in Jesus Christ,
His death and resurrection.

Why should I gain from His reward?
I cannot give an answer;
But this I know with all my heart –
His wounds have paid my ransom.

Upon the cross, the Savior suffered and died. But, the cross was not a scene of defeat for Christ. The cross was the location of ultimate victory. There, on Calvary's hill, Jesus died so that you might not. There, on the cross, the Savior bled and paid the ransom for your sin. Jesus was willing to be forsaken so that you could be restored. Jesus was abandoned by his Father so that you could be adopted.

The Old Testament encapsulates the law of God and tells of God's holiness and expectation. The Old Testament also speaks to us of the grace of God and the glory to come. The Old Testament points to the wisdom of God, which is folly to the world, but salvation to all who will believe.

At Christmas you tell stories of the words of angels

and shepherds. At Christmas you are reminded that the words and gifts of the wise men were treasured by Mary. It is appropriate and good to reflect upon the joy felt by Mary and even Elizabeth.[3] As you remember the manger and the virgin birth, do not neglect to consider the cross. The Son of God came to die so that you might live eternally and become sons and daughters of the Most High.

Jesus was born to die, and he died so that you could live, and that is the greatest gift ever conceived.

How does the cross impact the way you celebrate Christmas?

Prayer: God, as we celebrate the birth of our Savior, help me to reflect well upon his death this Christmas. Give me a heart and mind to better understand his sacrifice that enables us to have joy at Christmas.

---

[3] Luke 1:5-56

The Wisdom of God

"The Lord *possessed me at the beginning of his work, the first of his acts of old. Ages ago I was set up, at the first, before the beginning of the earth. When there were no depths I was brought forth, when there were no springs abounding with water. Before the mountains had been shaped, before the hills, I was brought forth, before he had made the earth with its fields, or the first of the dust of the world. When he established the heavens, I was there; when he drew a circle on the face of the deep, when he made firm the skies above, when he established the fountains of the deep, when he assigned to the sea its limit, so that the waters might not transgress his command, when he marked out the foundations of the earth,*

then I was beside him, like a master workman, and I was daily
his delight, rejoicing before him
always, rejoicing in his inhabited world and delighting
in the children of man.
Proverbs 8:22-31

Finding Christmas in the Old Testament is easier in some Scriptures than others. The prophetic passages of Isaiah, for instance, clearly proclaim the arrival of the Messiah. It is relatively easy to make a connection to Christ, even in the need for a king in the book of Judges, or in the promises to King David. The book of Proverbs seems to present a unique challenge, because there are no prophetic references to Christ, with some scholars suggesting that there are no allusions at all.

If all of Scripture ultimately points to Jesus, then even the Proverbs point to Christ. But, how?

The answer is not found in a scholarly work about the Bible or an archeological reference to King Solomon (who wrote many of the Proverbs). We find Jesus in the Proverbs by looking to the apostle Paul.

In an extended passage about the wisdom of God and the foolishness of man in 1 Corinthians, Paul refers to Christ as "the power of God and the wisdom of God."[1]

---

[1] 1 Corinthians 1:24

If Jesus is the personification of God's wisdom as Paul claims, then references to God's wisdom in the Proverbs are references to Christ. The Proverbs tell us that God's Wisdom (Christ) has always been with him, so the Proverbs teach us about the Trinity and the eternal nature of the Trinitarian relationship. The Proverbs teach us that the Father and the Son work in concert with one another, and that the Son takes delight in the children of man.

The Proverbs do not only speak of Wisdom as God's eternal companion, but they also urge humans to seek wisdom. Proverbs 3:13 promises blessing to those who find wisdom. Proverbs 2:4 urges, "Look for wisdom." Proverbs 4:5 commands, "Get wisdom." Taken together with Paul's words, we learn that Jesus is the personification of wisdom and Proverbs urges us to seek after wisdom, meaning that we should also seek after Jesus.

At Christmas, where I am from, it is common to see bumper stickers that say, "Wise men still seek him." Perhaps this is the best way to explain Christ in the Proverbs. Jesus is the fountain of wisdom and is the ultimate fulfillment of wisdom. The wise men who came from the east in search of the Messiah understood the great value of this One who had been foretold from time immemorial. He is still there to be found, and you are wise to seek him.

Christ is the wisdom of God. As such, he will often be perceived as foolish by the world, but your goal is not to conform to the world around you. Your goal is to be united with Christ. Your goal is to read his word, find God's wisdom, trust his teachings, and, in so doing to find eternal hope this Christmas season.

Finally, remember that the wisdom of God is not merely good advice. Jesus, the Wisdom of God, is not a pop-psychology social-media influencer. The Proverbs ultimately urge us to seek and find Christ, the hope of the world and the Savior of all mankind. He's there in the Proverbs, and he can be central in all of your celebrations this Christmas.

Why is the fear of the Lord the beginning of wisdom?

Prayer: Father, make me wise to seek you and wise to live for you. Give me wisdom to bring people to you and the ability to impart godly wisdom to others.

God Will Judge

The end of the matter; all has been heard. Fear God and keep his commandments, for this is the whole duty of man. For God will bring every deed into judgment, with every secret thing, whether good or evil.

Ecclesiastes 12:13-14

The book of Ecclesiastes, Job, Psalms, the Song of Solomon, and Proverbs are the wisdom literature of the Old Testament. The book of Ecclesiastes is largely pessimistic and should be understood through the lens of these last two verses. The end of the matter, for the author of Ecclesiastes, is that all of life is ultimately in

God's hands. As a result, we should all lean into the LORD and trust his heart and his commandments.

Stephen Covey was a businessman, educator, and self-help book author. In his most influential book, *The 7 Habits of Highly Effective People*, Covey identifies seven habits to help you to find success in life. The habits include "be proactive," and "think win-win."

Perhaps his most important piece of advice, however, is the habit of "beginning with the end in mind." As we consider Christmas in the Old Testament, Ecclesiastes gives us an opportunity to consider not only the book of Ecclesiastes, but also to consider Christmas with the end in mind. Christmas is a time for celebration and merry-making. Christmas is also a time to remember and reflect upon the goodness and grace of God who sent his Son into the world to die for our sins.

Christmas is a great time to begin with the end in mind.

The fact that God would, and did, send his son into the world to rescue sinners, is proof of God's love toward his creation. A God who would go to such great lengths to rescue his creation is one that should not be toyed with or considered lightly.

The same God who created the world and sent Christ into the world is the God who will one day bring all things to a conclusion. The same God who sent Jesus is the same God who will judge those who have rejected Christ. At Christmas, it is appropriate that you would not only celebrate Jesus, but also consider the end of all things—the day that you will stand before the Creator of the universe.

On that day, Christmas will not be a word on your lips or a thought in your mind. On that day, the only hope you have is that Jesus died to save you from your sins. On that day, your salvation will not be found in your Christmas celebrations or your worldly successes. On the day that you stand before God for judgment, your only hope is that you know Jesus and that he knows you.

This Christmas, begin with the end in mind.

The birth of Jesus is worthy of such grand celebration because he died and rose again. Jesus was born to die, died to rise, and rose to rescue all who would call upon his name. The birth of Jesus was the culmination of centuries of prophecy and promise, but it was not the end.

The birth of Jesus was the beginning of the end of Satan's dominance and sin's reign. The birth of Jesus was the beginning of the end of death and hell and pain. We come to Christmas with the end in mind—the end on the cross and the empty tomb, for sure, but even more. We come to Christmas with the end of *all* things in mind. We come to Christmas knowing that God is working all things together for our good and his glory. We come to Christmas knowing that the baby in a manger will one day be the king on a white horse,[1] and we celebrate him as such.

With that reality fresh in your heart and mind, what is your duty? Surrender your life fully to Christ who died to save you, fear God and keep his commandments, and live your life for his glory and for the good of those around you.

In the end, you can trust in the God who began with a plan to redeem you from your sin. In the end, you can trust in a Savior who was born in a manger. In the end, you can trust in Christ's sacrifice and God's grace to avoid judgment for your sin. That is worthy of the greatest of all celebrations.

How was the birth of Christ the beginning of God's restoration project? How does your salvation save you from God's judgment?

Prayer: God, thank you for sending Jesus to take the judgment for my sin. Help me to trust you through the process of making me more like you every day.

---

[1] Revelation 19:11-16

The Better Adam

*Therefore the LORD himself will give you a sign. Behold, the
virgin shall conceive and bear a son, and shall call his name
Immanuel. He shall eat curds and honey when he knows how
to refuse the evil and choose the good.*
Isaiah 7:14-15

After the reign of King Solomon, Israel teetered on the
verge of civil war. Following a time of unrest, the Kingdom
of Israel divided into two kingdoms. The Northern Kingdom
retained the name Israel. The Southern Kingdom, which
included Jerusalem, became Judah. Isaiah was a prophet
in Jerusalem when Judah was invaded by the Assyrians.
He was prophet who had access to the kings of Judah and

often spoke directly to them. In addition to speaking to the people and rulers of Judah, Isaiah also wrote down his prophecies, many of which have been collected into the book of Isaiah in the Old Testament.

Isaiah may be known more for his "one liners" than anything. Even people not familiar with Isaiah the prophet may have heard, "but they who wait for the LORD shall renew their strength; they shall mount up with wings like eagles; they shall run and not be weary; they shall walk and not faint." Those are Isaiah's words from Isaiah 40:31. Others have heard Isaiah 1:18, "'Come now, let us reason together,' says the LORD: 'though your sins are like scarlet, they shall be as white as snow; though they are red like crimson, they shall become like wool.'"

Most famously, however, Isaiah prophesied about the coming Messiah. At Christmas, Isaiah is one of the most quoted prophets of the Bible because he had so much to say about the Savior who would be born to the people of Israel. Isaiah wrote more than seven hundred years before Jesus was to be born, but he wrote in such a way that people then, as well as people today, read his words and grow eager with anticipation about the hope that God brings through his Messiah.

One of the great hopes promised through Isaiah might go unnoticed by many people reading this powerful book of prophecy. Isaiah writes in chapter 7 that God's Messiah—

his anointed Savior—would be called "Immanuel," and "He shall eat curds and honey when he knows how to refuse the evil and choose the good."

Immanuel is one of the great promises of hope in the Old Testament, because Immanuel literally means, "God with us." John 1 explains that when Isaiah prophesied about Immanuel, it was not figurative language. Jesus Christ, the living Word of God, literally came and lived among his people. He came to earth as God in the flesh and lived among his people. No longer would the people need the assurance of the temple to know that God loved them and was with them; God himself came and dwelt among them. Isaiah prophesied about Jesus as God in the flesh more than 700 years before Jesus was born.

Isaiah also spoke, in chapter 7, of the Messiah as one who knows "how to refuse evil and choose the good." Not only would Jesus come to be God among his people, the Messiah would also come and choose good and not evil. The Messiah was going to do the job that Adam was supposed to do in the beginning. In the beginning God created the heavens and earth and he created Adam and Eve and placed them in the Garden of Eden where they were to be God's people, in God's place, living obediently and joyfully under God's rule and blessing.[1]

Of course, Adam and Eve failed. When temptation came

---

[1] Genesis 1 and 2

and an opportunity presented itself for them to reject God's rule and choose their own sinful way, Adam and Eve chose evil and not good.[2] God's Messiah would be different. The Messiah represented hope and the presence of God. The Messiah also represented a new beginning for God's people. Adam rejected God's rule and God's blessing, but the anointed one of whom Isaiah spoke would be a new and better Adam. He would welcome God's rule. When Immanuel—God with us— encountered temptation, he would not rebel against the LORD; instead, he would trust God's goodness and welcome God's rule and blessing. God's Messiah would be the second and better Adam.

The Apostle Paul describes Jesus, God's Messiah, this way in Philippians 2:6-11:

> *Who, though he was in the form of God, did not count equality with God a thing to be grasped, but emptied himself, by taking the form of a servant, being born in the likeness of men. And being found in human form, he humbled himself by becoming obedient to the point of death, even death on a cross. Therefore God has highly exalted him and bestowed on him the name that is above every name, so that at the name of Jesus every knee should bow, in heaven and on earth and under the earth, and every tongue confess that Jesus Christ is LORD, to the glory of God the Father.*

---

[2] Genesis 3

Adam sinned, and since then, all other men and women have failed to live up to God's good plan. Except Jesus. Jesus is God's promise, and he is the hope you need. He is the better Adam who overcame temptation, and you can trust him.

As Christmas approaches, your thoughts of goodwill and peace on Earth may occasionally be interrupted by the reality of the sin and brokenness in the world around you—or even in your own life. The joy of Christmas can be overshadowed by the reality of suffering, but the promise of Isaiah is that Jesus is with us and that he is the perfect man, perfectly fulfilling God's good plan.

What things threaten to rob you of your joy this Christmas season? How can you find joy in Christ?

Prayer: God, help me to see hope in the midst of brokenness in the world around me. Put people in my path who need the hope of Christ and give me the courage to share that hope.

The Righteous Branch

Behold, the days are coming, declares the LORD, when I will
raise up for David a righteous Branch, and he shall reign as
king and deal wisely, and shall execute justice and righteous-
ness in the land. In his days Judah will be saved, and Israel
will dwell securely. And this is the name by which he will be
called: "The LORD is our righteousness."
Jeremiah 23:5-6

One of the great challenges of finding Jesus in the Old Testament is that readers in the twenty-first century do not have Old Testament experiences, expectations, or struggles. As you read the Old Testament today, you do not read it through Old Testament eyes. In fact, even as you read the New Testament texts about Jesus, you do not read through the eyes of a first-century middle easterner, but rather through the eyes of a Westerner in the twenty-first century.

In your church and in your Christian circles, you likely speak about Jesus regularly as "Lord and Savior." You may occasionally speak or sing about him as "King," but unless you have lived under authoritarian rulers, you probably do not have a great appreciation for the importance of a good king. The character and demeanor of a king shaped an entire kingdom. Thus, a good and righteous king is desirable because of his willingness to treat his people with fairness and dignity.

Jeremiah was known as the weeping prophet, and many scholars believe that he wrote the book of Jeremiah, as well as the books of Lamentations and First and Second Kings. Jeremiah was a reluctant prophet[1] tasked with warning the nation of Judah about God's coming judgment. But God, who is rich in mercy, did not only warn about his judgment; he gave Jeremiah words of encouragement so that the people of Judah would know that God's judgment would not last forever.

Jeremiah 23:5-6 represents some of those words of encouragement. God's people (the nation of Judah) were under God's judgment because they turned to idols instead

---

[1]Jeremiah 1:6

of trusting in the one true God. God—and, by extension, God's prophets—held the kings of Judah particularly responsible for their sinful leadership whereby they led Judah to sin. God's people were led astray in part because they had kings who steered them away from living under God's rule and God's blessing.

With that in mind, God gives a promise to his people who are experiencing his judgment. The day will come when God's judgment would end, and, in that day, God would raise up a good king. Jeremiah specifically refers to this person as a righteous Branch. The imagery of Christ as a branch is born out of the idea that the line of David is represented as a tree, and the righteous Branch would be a ruler—a king who would judge and rule wisely. God would not only bring his people back home one day, he would also give them the king they needed.

Of course, what the people of Jeremiah's day could not have understood is that the king God would give would be God in the flesh. He would be the righteous king, the perfect prophet, and the chief high priest. In one person, Jesus is the prophet, priest, and king that all the other Old Testament heroes could only point to. The people of Jeremiah's day looked forward to a king who would rule them well. What God gave, however, was not only a king who would govern, but also a savior who would deliver them in this life and the life to come.

As you look for Jesus in Jeremiah, consider that the weeping prophet spoke of a coming king who would wipe away every tear.[2] That king is Jesus, and this Christmas, you can hope in his righteous rule and divine deliverance.

How does your understanding of Jesus as the just and righteous King give you hope when you or your loved ones experience pain?

Prayer: Jesus, help me to trust you as my King for deliverance from hurt and pain.

---

[2] Revelation 21:4

Dry Bones Shall Live

The hand of the L<small>ORD</small> was upon me, and he brought me out in the Spirit of the L<small>ORD</small> and set me down in the middle of the valley; it was full of bones. And he led me around among them, and behold, there were very many on the surface of the valley, and behold, they were very dry. And he said to me, "Son of man, can these bones live?" And I answered, "O L<small>ORD</small> God, you know." Then he said to me, "Prophesy over these bones, and say to them, O dry bones, hear the word of the L<small>ORD</small>. Thus says the L<small>ORD</small> God to these bones: Behold, I will cause breath to enter you, and you shall live. And I will lay sinews upon you, and will cause flesh to come upon you, and

cover you with skin, and put breath in you, and you shall live,
and you shall know that I am the LORD."
Ezekiel 37:1-6

Ezekiel prophesied to God's people while they were living in exile in Babylon. Because of their sin, God removed them from the Promised Land and were living in a foreign nation. God's people had rejected God's rule and God's blessing, and they had been expelled from God's Land. In such a terrible situation, it could be easy to believe that God had forgotten and abandoned his people.

Perhaps you have found yourself feeling abandoned at some point in your Christian journey. Have you ever felt as though God doesn't hear your prayers, or perhaps that God has given up you on you? Maybe you have felt that your sin has done so much damage to your relationship with the Lord that God will never love you again. If so, then you know what it is like to live in exile and to feel surrounded by dead, dry bones.

The good news is that God's promise to his people through Ezekiel is his promise to you as well.

As Ezekiel was praying, the LORD carried him away in a vision to a valley of dry bones. A valley where a great army had been slain. In that place of death and destruction, the LORD asked Ezekiel one simple question, "Can these bones live?" Ezekiel's answer was one of faith instead of fear. Rather than speaking about the reality of dead, dry bones, Ezekiel was focused on the mercy and grace of a living, powerful God.

The LORD told Ezekiel to speak to the bones and watch them come to life. Why? Because God's promise to Israel was that she had not been wholly forgotten. God's people were living in exile, living under God's judgment, but they would not be there forever. God had disciplined his children, but he had not forgotten them. Though they felt dry and dead, there was life and hope.

The source of Israel's life was not found in Israel, but in the God of Israel and in the power of his Word. Just as the LORD created life from nothing in the beginning, the Word of the LORD would bring life to Israel. In Ezekiel, we see Christ in the spoken Word of God over dead, dry bones.

John 1 teaches that the Word of God was the instrument of creation in the beginning. John also explains that this Word of God was God. Jesus, the Word of God, "became flesh and dwelt among us."[1] The Word of God who brought life to the valley of dry bones came to earth in the person of Jesus Christ to bring the dead to life. Jesus is the living Word of God. Ezekiel prophesied the Word of God, but in Jesus, the Word has come to live among us.

As you look toward Christmas, know that the God who

---

[1] John 1:14

brought life out of death in Ezekiel, is the same God who can bring hope out of the dark places in your life. Even if on this day you feel separated from the LORD, he is as close as a prayer. The Word that brought life then is the Word that can bring life to you today. Run to God's Word and find hope and healing for the dry places in your soul. In Isaiah 43:19, God promised, "Behold, I am doing a new thing; now it springs forth, do you not perceive it? I will make a way in the wilderness and rivers in the desert."

There is hope. There is life. There are even rivers in the desert, because God is concerned for your soul!

How has the Word of God brought healing in your life?

Prayer: God, thank you for your Word that brings life from death and wholeness from brokenness. Help me to hide your Word in my heart and to be changed by your Word as it renews my mind.

God in the Fire

Then Nebuchadnezzar was filled with fury, and the expression of his face was changed against Shadrach, Meshach, and Abednego. He ordered the furnace heated seven times more than it was usually heated. And he ordered some of the mighty men of his army to bind Shadrach, Meshach, and Abednego, and to cast them into the burning fiery furnace. Then these men were bound in their cloaks, their tunics, their hats, and their other garments, and they were thrown into the burning fiery furnace. Because the king's order was urgent and the furnace overheated, the flame of the fire killed those men who took up Shadrach, Meshach, and Abednego. And these three men, Shadrach, Meshach, and Abednego, fell bound into the burning fiery furnace. Then King Nebuchad-

nezzar was astonished and rose up in haste. He declared to
his counselors, "Did we not cast three men bound into the
fire?" They answered and said to the king, "True, O king." He
answered and said, "But I see four men unbound, walking in
the midst of the fire, and they are not hurt; and the appear-
ance of the fourth is like a son of the gods."
Daniel 3:19-25

In some Old Testament books, Jesus seems to be dropping little hints waiting for us to notice him, as in the gentle whisper of the LORD to Elijah after the storm.[1] In other places, Jesus' presence is so obvious that it is difficult to not smile at his willingness to pull back the curtain of his divinity long enough for ordinary humans to gaze upon him.

The book of Daniel tells the story of one of those very obvious appearances of Jesus, as the LORD intervenes in the plans of King Nebuchadnezzar and saves the lives of three young Hebrew men. Shadrach, Meshach, and Abednego had been deported to Babylon and had become part of the king's court. Essentially, they were being culturally indoctrinated and groomed for leadership in Babylon. Part of the expectation was for these young men, along with everyone else in Babylon, to bow down and worship before a golden idol Nebuchadnezzar had commissioned.

---

[1] 1 Kings 19:9-13

Because Shadrach, Meshach, and Abednego were committed to the God of Israel, they refused to worship the idol and were subsequently cast into a burning fiery furnace. Most sermons and lessons about these three young men focus on their faith and their commitment to the Lord illustrated in their statement to King Nebuchadnezzar in Daniel 3:17-18,

> If this be so, our God whom we serve is able to deliver us from the burning fiery furnace, and he will deliver us out of your hand, O king. But if not, be it known to you, O king, that we will not serve your gods or worship the golden image that you have set up."

The faith of these young men is more than commendable. However, as you reflect upon the story of Shadrach, Meshach, and Abednego this Christmas season, look for Christ in the story. He is not hard to find, because he's in the middle of the story, and he is visible to everyone.

When Nebuchadnezzar and his aides looked in, there was no doubt that the God of Shadrach, Meshach, and Abednego was the true God. They cast three men into the fire, but there was a fourth walking with them—and the fourth had an appearance "like a son of the gods." The presence of Christ in this story was not only an experiential presence felt by his people; even the pagans persecuting God's people were made aware of the presence of Christ in their midst.

But take another look at the story. Where was Christ? Where was the manifest presence of God seen?

Shadrach, Meshach, and Abednego did not experience the full outpouring of God's presence until they stepped into the fire. As you find time to sit by roaring fires or enjoy candlelit meals this Christmas season, take time to reflect on the appearance of Christ in the fire. It is normal to desire a relatively comfortable life, but often Christ's presence is made most manifest in the difficult seasons of life.

In the fires of life, you may experience Christ's love and protection more intimately than at any other time. In those times, the watching world may learn more of Christ's care for you than they ever have in your times of ease and comfort. Even on that first Christmas, Jesus entered the world in the middle of Mary and Joseph's fire. Imagine their circumstance—a baby, born to a virgin. There is no easy explanation, there is only struggle and fear. And yet, in the middle of that fiery furnace, the Lord of Life was born to bring peace to all who would trust him.

In the middle of their trial, Mary and Joseph experienced the presence of God. Your trials are opportunities for God's goodness to shine bright—even at Christmas.

When has God sustained you with his presence through a difficult time in your life?

Prayer: God, help me to walk into difficult trials with confidence that you are with me. Help me to trust your heart to care for me, even when I can't see your hand of protection.

A Savior for Us All

And it shall come to pass afterward, that I will pour out my Spirit on all flesh; your sons and your daughters shall prophesy, your old men shall dream dreams, and your young men shall see visions. Even on the male and female servants in those days I will pour out my Spirit. And I will show wonders in the heavens and on the earth, blood and fire and columns of smoke. The sun shall be turned to darkness, and the moon to blood, before the great and awesome day of the LORD comes. And it shall come to pass that everyone who calls on the name of the LORD shall be saved. For in Mount Zion and in

Jerusalem there shall be those who escape, as the Lord has
said, and among the survivors shall be
those whom the Lord calls.
Joel 2:28-32

Shortly after Jesus told his disciples that he would be betrayed and killed, he promised them that he would not leave them alone. He promised, "I will ask the Father, and he will give you another Helper to be with you forever, even the Spirit of truth, whom the world cannot receive, because it neither sees him nor knows him ... . "[1] The promise of the Holy Spirit would find its fulfillment in Acts 2 when the Holy Spirit came upon Jesus' disciples. Since that day, the Holy Spirit of God has been a wonderful indwelling gift of God to all of his children who have called on the name of the Lord for salvation.

However, the Holy Spirit was not an afterthought from the Lord. As you continue your journey in the Old Testament toward Christmas, you can see God's promise of the Holy Spirit from the prophet Joel. For Old Testament believers, this promise was an incredible gift to consider. Up to this point in time, only particular individuals were blessed with the presence of the Holy Spirit in special situations. In the story of Samson, for instance, the Spirit of God would rush upon Samson and he would perform

---

[1] John 14:16-17

incredible feats of strength.[2] In other situations, the Spirit of God would empower prophets to prophesy God's Word.

The greatest hope in the book of Joel was the universal nature of God's promise given through Joel. God was going to do such a great work that his name would be known in all the earth, and all who would call upon his name would be saved. No longer would God's people be confined to a specific place; instead, as God poured his Spirit out upon the world, God's people would experience his place and his blessing anywhere they encountered his Spirit.

In Joel, God promised to completely turn the world upside down for one great purpose: to save men, women, boys, and girls from all over the world, and to fill them with his Holy Spirit. No longer would God's special blessing be reserved for a few people—God's indwelling presence would be available to *all* of God's people.

The fulfillment of Joel's prophecy came in Acts 2—there we read about how the Holy Spirit came to Christ's disciples as they were praying in a big room in Jerusalem after Jesus had ascended back to the Father in heaven. After Jesus' disciples were filled with the Holy Spirit, Peter stood up and preached the gospel and about three thousand people were saved that day.

The Holy Spirit came to assure God's people of his

---

[2] Judges 13-16

presence, but also to empower God's people to proclaim the good news of the gospel. The Holy Spirit's presence ensured that all of God's people could obey the Great Commission and preach the good news of Jesus because all of God's people have God's special indwelling presence.

The promise of Joel and it's fulfillment in the book of Acts means that you also, as a follower of Christ, have the presence of God's Holy Spirit in you, and that is a wonderful gift that you can celebrate at Christmas.

How does the Holy Spirit give you comfort and confidence? How has God's indwelling presence empowered you to proclaim the gospel?

Prayer: Lord, thank you for fulfilling your promise to Joel through Jesus Christ. Thank you for the gift of the Holy Spirit.

The God Who Forgives

Who is a God like you, pardoning iniquity and passing over transgression for the remnant of his inheritance? He does not retain his anger forever, because he delights in steadfast love. He will again have compassion on us; he will tread our iniquities underfoot. You will cast all our sins into the depths of the sea. You will show faithfulness to Jacob and steadfast love to Abraham, as you have sworn to our fathers from the days of old.
Micah 7:18-20

God has always been a forgiving God. In the Garden of Eden, after Adam and Eve sinned, God created for them clothes made out of animal skins. God sacrificed part of his creation to cover the sins of Adam and Eve.[1] When God revealed himself to Moses on Mt. Sinai, part of his self-declaration in Exodus 34:6-7 was to describe himself as, "The LORD, the LORD, a God merciful and gracious, slow to anger, and abounding in steadfast love and faithfulness, keeping steadfast love for thousands, forgiving iniquity and transgression and sin."

The prophet Micah was from a rural area, but his prophecies were directed mostly toward the capital city of Jerusalem. The LORD gave Micah the task of going to Jerusalem, the center of Israel's power and government, to speak words of warning and future destruction. However, even in the midst of his words of woe, Micah's prophecies are sprinkled with hope.

Micah 5:2-5a is the most quoted section of the book at Christmas time,

> *But you, O Bethlehem Ephrathah, who are too little to be among the clans of Judah, from you shall come forth for me one who is to be ruler in Israel, whose coming forth is from of old, from ancient days. Therefore he shall give them up until the time when she who is in labor has given birth; then the rest of his brothers shall return to the people of Israel. And he shall stand and shepherd his flock in the strength of the LORD, in the*

---

[1] Genesis 3

majesty of the name of the LORD his God. And they shall dwell secure, for now he shall be great to the ends of the earth. And he shall be their peace.

Micah's prophecy is an important key to understanding Jesus as the Messiah. It was no accident that Mary and Joseph went up to Bethlehem to be taxed and were there when Jesus was born. It was the divine plan of God that his Messiah would be born in Bethlehem and it was God's plan that a prophet *from a small town* would announce the coming birth of the Messiah *in a small town*.

It does not matter where you come from. God can use you.

As you celebrate Christmas this year, notice more out of Micah than the prophecy of Bethlehem. Remember the hope found in Micah's words. God was not only sending a shepherd to be born from David's city; God was sending a healer to pardon and forgive. God has always been a compassionate God, but when you are living under God's heavy hand of judgment, it can be easy to forget his love.

Micah sent word to God's people that he would not always be angry with them. Psalm 30:5 says, "Weeping may tarry for the night, but joy comes with the morning." The hope spelled out by Micah was to come with the morning. There were dark days for Jerusalem, but the light of hope would dawn anew and God's people would again experience his mercy and grace.

The hope of Christmas from Micah is the promise of God's continued love and faithfulness. The faithfulness he had shown to the Patriarchs would be even more evident in the work of Christ. Christ was born to be the sacrifice for the sins of mankind. The promise of forgiveness was given seven hundred years before the prophecies of Jesus were fulfilled through his birth, death, and resurrection. The forgiveness of your sins is the greatest gift that God offers you, not only at Christmas, but at any time and for anyone who calls upon the name of the Lord.

How does fulfilled prophecy give you greater confidence to trust the teachings of the Bible?

Prayer: God, thank you for the hope given in Micah's prophecy and the salvation that was achieved by Christ's sacrifice on the cross.

A Fountain for Cleansing

And I will pour out on the house of David and the inhabitants of Jerusalem a spirit of grace and pleas for mercy, so that, when they look on me, on him whom they have pierced, they shall mourn for him, as one mourns for an only child, and weep bitterly over him, as one weeps over a firstborn. On that day the mourning in Jerusalem will be as great as the mourning for Hadad-rimmon in the plain of Megiddo. The land shall mourn, each family by itself: the family of the house of David by itself, and their wives by themselves; the family of the house of Nathan by itself, and their wives by themselves; the family of the house of Levi by itself, and their wives by themselves; the family of the Shimeites by itself, and their wives by themselves; and all the families that are left, each by

itself, and their wives by themselves. On that day there shall
be a fountain opened for the house of David and the inhabit-
ants of Jerusalem, to cleanse them from sin and uncleanness.
Zechariah 12:10-13:1

"There is a Fountain Filled with Blood"[1] is one of the best known English hymns of the Christian church:

> *There is a fountain filled with blood*
> *Drawn from Emmanuel's veins;*
> *And sinners, plunged beneath that flood,*
> *Lose all their guilty stains.*

> *The dying thief rejoiced to see*
> *That fountain in his day;*
> *And there have I, as vile as he,*
> *Washed all my sins away.*

> *Dear dying Lamb, thy precious blood*
> *Shall never lose its power;*
> *Till all the ransomed church of God*
> *Be saved to sin no more.*

> *E'er since, by faith, I saw the stream*
> *Thy flowing wounds supply,*
> *Redeeming love has been my theme,*
> *And shall be till I die.*

---

[1] William Cowper, "There is a Fountain Filled with Blood," 1772.

The hymn was written published in 1772 by William Cowper. Cowper (pronounced "Cooper") was an Englishman and was a close friend of John Newton, who wrote "Amazing Grace." Perhaps most striking is that Cowper was a man who suffered greatly under depression and bouts of utter despair. Cowper attempted suicide several times over the course of his adult life.

Cowper was first drawn to the LORD by reading the story of Jesus raising Lazarus from the dead, and was finally converted after reading Romans 3:25: "Whom God hath set forth to be a propitiation through faith in his blood, to declare his righteousness for the remission of sins that are past, through the forbearance of God" (KJV). Upon reading these words, Cowper came to understand that the sacrifice of Christ's death on the cross was sufficient to bring about the forgiveness of his sins. He was saved while a patient in an insane asylum.

He would soon make his way to Olney where John Newton was his pastor. Under Newton's tutelage and encouragement, Cowper put the glories of God to song and poem.

The inspiration for "There is a Fountain Filled with Blood" was Zechariah 13:1. As Cowper learned of God's promises in the Old Testament, he testified to God's fulfillment in the New Testament. For William Cowper, the cleansing power of God was not an academic consideration.

Just as the thief upon the cross found forgiveness through the shed blood of Jesus, so, too, had Cowper discovered this forgiveness, and he could write, not merely as a student, but as a recipient.

On this Christmas Eve, as you enjoy time with family and friends, reflect upon the complete cleansing that is possible through Jesus Christ. Perhaps nothing in creation looks as clean as fresh-fallen snow. A grimy city-scape can be transformed overnight into a beautiful, blank canvas with a few inches of frozen precipitation. The world seems new with a fresh covering of snow.

The forgiveness that Jesus promises is more than just a covering or ignoring sin. Jesus forgives, and then renews. He takes dead old hearts and makes them alive and new. Jesus takes the broken and makes it well. At Christmas, we celebrate the day Jesus was born and the difference it made in the world. Do not neglect to reflect upon the day you were reborn, and the new life you have been given through Christ:

> *And you were dead in the trespasses and sins in which you once walked, following the course of this world, following the prince of the power of the air, the spirit that is now at work in the sons of disobedience— among whom we all once lived in the passions of our flesh, carrying out the desires of the body and the mind, and were by nature children of wrath, like the rest of man-*

kind. But God, being rich in mercy, because of the great love with which he loved us, even when we were dead in our trespasses, made us alive together with Christ.[2]

What was the most significant change in your life after being made new in Christ?

Prayer: Thank you, God, for the fountain of Christ's blood that brought about the forgiveness of sin. Thank you that sinners, just like me, can be made clean, whole, and new.

---

[2] Ephesians 2:1-5

The God Who Heals

*For behold, the day is coming, burning like an oven, when all the arrogant and all evildoers will be stubble. The day that is coming shall set them ablaze, says the L*ORD *of hosts, so that it will leave them neither root nor branch. But for you who fear my name, the sun of righteousness shall rise with healing in its wings. You shall go out leaping like calves from the stall. And you shall tread down the wicked, for they will be ashes under the soles of your feet, on the day when I act, says the* L*ORD of hosts. Remember the law of my servant Moses, the statutes and rules that I commanded him at Horeb for all Israel. Behold, I will send you Elijah the prophet before the great and awesome day of the* L*ORD comes. And he will turn the hearts of fathers to their children and the hearts of*

children to their fathers, lest I come and strike the land with a
decree of utter destruction.
Malachi 4:1-6

As you read this on Christmas Day, many of you are parents who have spent the last day preparing gifts, giving gifts, replacing batteries, assembling furniture and toys, and trying to catch a nap. Some of you are fathers, and if you are a father and have spent time with your children, you are part of the fulfillment of prophecy.

When the time came for Malachi to deliver his prophecy, he was the last of the Minor Prophets and his book became the last book in the Old Testament. Malachi spoke of judgment and doom. He spoke of the Day of the LORD. Many in Malachi's day expected the Day of the LORD to be a day when God would judge the nations around Israel and return Israel's monarchy to a position of power. However, God's plan was different and he would use the arrival of Jesus Christ to initiate the Day of the LORD.

If the Old Testament were a movie, Malachi would be the cliffhanger at the end. When you read Malachi, two things occur to you. First, you know there is more to come. Second, you long for the fulfillment of all that Malachi promised. Malachi ends with a longing for something better—a longing for Christ.

Israel longed for God to destroy her national enemies,

but God knows the destructive power of sin. Israel did not need to be rescued from other nations, Israel needed to be restored to their God. Malachi offered hope that a Savior would come to restore God's people.

Malachi promised something that many people long for even today. He promised that the Day of the LORD would come, and he promised that on that day, God would "turn the hearts of fathers to their children and the hearts of children to their fathers."

Don't miss it.

The family is God's first institution and it is often the first place Satan attacks. The restoration of the family represented God's power over sin and Israel's turn toward God.

Broken families are ongoing evidence of Satan's destructive power. It is heart-breaking to see fathers who do not care for their children and the sadness that results in children turning away from their fathers. But God's promise through Malachi is that broken things will be repaired.

Where does God begin his work of restoration?

When he changes the hearts of people, a change in the way they interact with their families should be evident.

At Christmas, we celebrate family, and that is not an

accident. Christmas is a taste of the greater promise of God to heal families and restore hope. As you long for time with your family today—and as you enjoy it—give thanks to the God who desires to heal broken families and strengthen healthy ones.

But what of those living in the midst of broken families? Does God's promise not apply to them?

God promised through Malachi to change the hearts of fathers and of children. God's promise certainly included mothers and daughters as well as sons and fathers, but this was more than a statement about the nuclear family. When Jesus came, he instituted his church as a new kind of family for his followers[1]—a family united by the gospel of Jesus Christ. Jesus came to give a family to even those who had been rejected by their relatives.

God's promise was also about the reign of peace and prosperity. The promise of Malachi mirrors the promise of Isaiah that the Prince of Peace would be born.

God was promising that when Christ came, hearts turned toward him would no longer be focused on selfish striving, war, and destruction. Christ was coming to change hearts and lives. Obviously, there is only partial fulfillment today of that promise. There is hope, because all who call upon Jesus for salvation find peace—however, wars still

---

[1] Matthew 16:18

rage and families still fall apart. There is coming a day when Christ returns, and on that day, wars will cease and there will be no more tears.[2]

He is the God who heals, and that healing is complete and total. On this Christmas Day, praise the God who restores families. Praise the Prince of Peace who ends wars and striving. Praise the Savior who died to forgive sinners and to restore them to a relationship with their Heavenly Father.

On this day, give glory to God in the highest, because the peace he brings to earth starts in hearts and homes and one-on-one relationships. As you pray for peace around the world, pray also for peace in your own home and community, and celebrate the hope of healthy families that God brings.

Thank God for turning his heart of love toward you and for turning your sinful heart toward him. Thank God for Jesus who lived and died so that you could be saved. It is the greatest of God's gifts.

---

[2] Revelation 21:4

What is the most powerful display of a father's love you have ever seen?

Prayer: God, on this Christmas Day, thank you for being my Heavenly Father. Please be present to the fatherless, and turn the hearts of fathers toward their children. God, heal hearts and restore families.

A Note from the Author

Thank you for spending your Christmas season with me. It is my hope and prayer that you have grown in your understanding of who Jesus is and how the Old Testament points to him. For some of you, your time in this book may have helped you to understand that you know about Jesus, but you do not know Jesus as your personal Lord and Savior.

If you are interested in taking the next step with Jesus, please continue to read below about what a Christian is and how you can become a Christian today.

What is a Christian? You may have been led to believe that a Christian is someone who was born into a Christian family. Perhaps you think a Christian is someone who attends church. If you watch enough news, you might even believe that a Christian is someone who lives in a particular place or votes in a particular way. The Bible doesn't define Christianity in any of these ways.

When Paul and Silas were miraculously freed from prison in a city called Philippi, their jailer asked excitedly, "What must I do to be saved?" Paul and Silas responded with a simple answer, "Believe in the Lord Jesus, and you will be saved."

> About midnight Paul and Silas were praying and singing hymns to God, and the prisoners were listening to them, and suddenly there was a great earthquake, so that the foundations of the prison were shaken. And immediately all the doors were opened, and everyone's bonds were unfastened. When the jailer woke and saw that the prison doors were open, he drew his sword and was about to kill himself, supposing that the prisoners had escaped. But Paul cried with a loud voice, "Do not harm yourself, for we are all here." And the jailer called for lights and rushed in, and trembling with fear he fell down before Paul and Silas. Then he brought them out and said, "Sirs, what must I do to be saved?" And they said, "Believe in the Lord Jesus, and you will be saved, you and your household." And they spoke the word of the Lord to him and to all who were in his house. And he took them the same hour of the night and washed their wounds; and he was baptized at once, he and all his

family. Then he brought them up into his house and set food before them. And he rejoiced along with his entire household that he had believed in God. [1]

According to Paul and Silas in Acts 16, a Christian is a person who has believed in the name of the Lord Jesus for salvation.

Following a sermon in Acts chapter 2, the Apostle Peter was asked a similar question in verse 37. Those who had heard him preach asked, "Brothers, what shall we do?" He responded by saying,

Repent and be baptized every one of you in the name of Jesus Christ for the forgiveness of your sins, and you will receive the gift of the Holy Spirit.[2]

It may seem on the surface as though Paul and Peter are giving two different answers, but they are actually giving the same answer from two different directions. A person can't believe in Jesus for salvation until they have repented of their sin. To repent means to turn away from your old way of living. Being baptized was a public act affirming their belief in Jesus Christ.

So, what is a Christian? A Christian is a person who has

---

[1] Acts 16:25-34
[2] Acts 2:38

turned from their old, sinful way of living and trusted in Jesus Christ for salvation from their sins.

You may ask, why does anyone need to be saved and how does Jesus save them?

According to the book of Genesis in the Bible, God created the first human beings, Adam and Eve, and placed them in a garden paradise, called Eden. There in The Garden of Eden, Adam and Eve had everything they needed. They lived in perfect harmony with the world around them, with each other, and with their Creator. In that Garden, God gave Adam and Eve everything they needed, but he also gave them freedom to choose his way or another path. In Genesis 2, God warned them that to disobey him would bring death.

Rather than trusting in God, Adam and Eve trusted Satan and disobeyed God. As a result of that first sin, death and pain entered the world. Adam and Eve's sin meant that they no longer lived in perfect harmony with each other and their relationship with their Creator was fractured. Even their relationship with nature was damaged—rather than living in harmony with nature, they lived in a created world that seemed to oppose them at every turn.

Since that first sin, all of humanity has suffered the same fate. But you already knew that. No one has to tell you that the world is broken. You have seen hurt and pain. You have probably experienced death and heartache. Sin is a disease that runs through the human race, causing suffering and pain. Romans 3:23 says it this way, "All have sinned and fallen short of the glory of God." Just like with Adam and Eve, your sin and the sins of others separate you from God and the people you love. Your sin is a cosmic offense that makes you an enemy of God. Romans 6:23 says that because of sin, we all deserve death.

You know the world is broken, but it can be difficult to understand that you are a part of that broken system. Through Adam and Eve, sin entered the world. You were born into sin, but it can seem hard to believe that your sin is such a cosmic crime that it deserves death. Sin is so egregious because God is so perfect and holy. God is good and he desires what is best for you. When you sin, you rebel against your Creator, so we all are just as guilty of sin as Adam and Eve.

God was not finished with Adam and Eve when they sinned, and he is not finished with you. You have sinned and you deserve death, but God desires to give you life instead. Above, you only read half of Romans 6:23. The entire verse says, "For the wages of sin is death, but the free gift of God is eternal life."

You deserve death, but Jesus died to give you life instead. In John 3:16, Jesus told a man named Nicodemus,

For God so loved the world, that he gave his only Son, that whoever believes in him should not perish but have eternal life.

God loved the world—and you—so much that he sent Jesus to rescue you from your sin. Romans 5:8 says it this way, "but God shows his love for us in that while we were still sinners, Christ died for us."

Even though you were his enemy, Jesus died to set you free from the punishment for your sin. How can you experience this salvation? Romans 10:9 says, "Because, if you confess with your mouth that Jesus is Lord and believe in your heart that God raised him from the dead, you will be saved."

A Christian is a person who has believed in Jesus Christ's life, death, and resurrection and has asked Jesus to come into their life and save them. Romans 5:1 promises, "Therefore, since we have been justified by faith, we have peace with God through our Lord Jesus Christ." Romans 8:1 says, "There is therefore now no condemnation for those who are in Christ Jesus."

All of that means that when you confess Jesus as your Savior and Lord, you are set free. There is peace between you and God and there is no longer anything to condemn you. Jesus forgives you for your sin and reconciles you to God.

A Christian is a person who has been set free from their sins through a relationship with Jesus. But that isn't all. Jesus' final command to his disciples is called the Great Commission. When Jesus gave the Great Commission in Matthew 28:19, he commanded them to, "Go therefore and make disciples of all nations, baptizing them in the name of the Father and of the Son and of the Holy Spirit, teaching them to observe all that I have commanded you."

A Christian is a person who has been saved by Jesus and who seeks to live their life according to Jesus' example and commands.

Jesus never called his followers Christians. During Jesus' time on earth, his followers were normally called disciples. Jesus even referred to them as friends. When you try to picture what a Christian is, remember a Christian is a disciple or friend of Jesus. A Christian is a person who has been saved by Jesus, who wants to be around Jesus, and who wants to be like Jesus.

Are you a friend of Jesus? Has there been a time in your life when you have asked Jesus to save you from your sins and to become your Lord and Savior? If not, then pray today and ask God to save you and make you his disciple. There are no special words that you need to speak in order for God to save you, just pray to him. He promises in 1 John 1:9, "If we confess our sins, he is faithful and just to forgive us our sins and to cleanse us from all unrighteousness."

If you are a little unsure how to pray and ask God to save you, consider the following prayer below as a guide:

God, my life is broken because of my sin. I need you. I believe Jesus came to die and was raised from the grave to rescue the world from sin. I believe he even died to save me. Forgive me. Help me to turn from my sinful and selfish ways. Help me to put my trust in you. I know that Jesus is Lord of all, and I ask that Jesus save me from my sin right now and become Lord of my life. Help me to follow you in a relationship from this day on.

If you prayed this prayer, tell your pastor or the person who gave you this book. If you don't have a church home, contact us at Info@MakeItOrdinary.org and we can help you take your next steps.

Books & Resources

AVAILABLE FROM THE AUTHOR

VINTAGE CHRISTMAS

The birth of Jesus was prophesied, predicted, foreshadowed, and foretold in the Old Testament. The Old Testament points to Jesus, and Vintage Christmas celebrate Christmas a little differently this year as you understand your Savior more intimately and learn to love the Bible more fully.

Available on Amazon. Purchase links can be found at MakeItOrdinary.org

Through twenty-five devotions, you will grow in your understanding of Jesus through the lens of the Old Testament. Each day's devotion ends with a question to ponder and a short prayer—making it perfect for individual, family, or small group study.

HOME FOR THE HOLIDAYS

Home for the Holidays is an Advent devotional that will help you restore hope, love, joy, and peace in your home this Christmas season as you direct your attention to the Savior who was born to rescue the world from the curse of sin.

Available on Amazon. Purchase links can be found at MakeItOrdinary.org.

Written for families, the devotions are easy to follow and include scripture, discussion guides, activities, songs, and weekly challenges that you can complete together. You will be encouraged to focus on Christ and to share what you learn with one another and with others outside of your home.

NEXT STEPS

Becoming part of a church family is a significant decision that should not be taken lightly. As a member of a church, you commit to a spiritual family that provides care, encouragement, accountability, and support for one another, centered around God's Word.

Available on Amazon. Purchase links can be found at MakeItOrdinary.org.

We want to be open and honest about what we believe and how we work together as a church for the glory of God and the advancement of His kingdom. Individuals and churches can utilize the resources in this book to learn more about belonging to a healthy church family.

RAISED TO LIFE

If you are a new Christian, you are probably asking the question, "Now what?" The Bible gives you the answer for that, and this short guide for new believers will help you understand the answers to some of your questions.

Available on Amazon. Purchase links can be found at MakeItOrdinary.org.

Written for new believers, this guide will answer about the Christian faith, baptism, the need for a church family and small group accountability, and guide you in sharing your testimony. Also included is a guide for how to study Scripture using the 4 Es.

PODCASTS

The Ordinary Christian Podcast is a podcast dedicated to real people like you, seeking to love out your Christian faith in the ordinary aspects of everyday life.

Listen where you stream podcasts or at MakeItOrdinary.org.

The purpose of the 7-STRONG podcast is to share testimonies and tips to equip you with implementing seven habits that make you stronger and more resilient.

Listen where you stream podcasts or at 7-STRONG.org.

ORDINARY VIRTUES & 7-STRONG

The purpose of the virtue initiative is build character outside of the church through the teaching of traditional virtues and intentional mentoring in schools, teams, secular organizations, businesses, and the corporate world.

For more information, visit MakeItOrdinary.org.

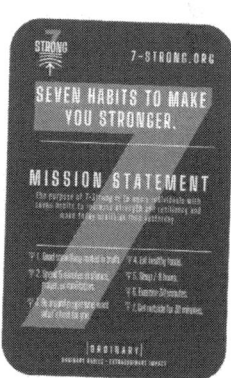

The purpose of the 7-Strong initiative is to equip individuals with seven habits to increase strength and resiliency and make today healthier than yesterday.

For more information, visit 7-STRONG.org.

Made in the USA
Columbia, SC
06 November 2024

45320315R00088